MASTERING
YOUR KEY ACCOUNTS

Maximize relationships
Create strategic partnerships
Increase sales

Stephan Schiffman

Avon, Massachusetts

Published by
Adams Media, an F+W Publications Company
57 Littlefield Street
Avon, MA 02322
www.adamsmedia.com

ISBN 10: 1-59337-534-4
ISBN 13: 978-1-59337-534-8

Printed in the United States of America.

J I H G F E D C B A

Library of Congress Cataloging-in-Publication Data
Schiffman, Stephan.
Mastering your key accounts / Stephan Schiffman.
p.   cm.
Includes index.
ISBN-13: 978-1-59337-534-8
ISBN-10: 1-59337-534-4
1. Selling--Key accounts. I. Title.
HF5438.8.K48S35 2007
658.85--dc22
2006028543

This publication is designed to provide accurate and authoritative information
with regard to the subject matter covered. It is sold with the understanding
that the publisher is not engaged in rendering legal, accounting, or other
professional advice. If legal advice or other expert assistance is required, the
services of a competent professional person should be sought.
—From a *Declaration of Principles* jointly adopted by a Committee of the
American Bar Association and a Committee of Publishers and Associations

Many of the designations used by manufacturers and sellers to distinguish
their product are claimed as trademarks. Where those designations appear in
this book and Adams Media was aware of a trademark claim, the designations
have been printed with initial capital letters.

This book is available at quantity discounts for bulk purchases.
For information, please call 1-800-289-0963.

Dedicated to SHS and AFS

CONTENTS

Part I
The Basics

<hr>**Part II**<hr>
The System

____ Part III ____
The Major Account

____ Part IV ____
The Right Relationships,
The Right Information

___ Appendices ___

PREFACE

This book, even more than others I have written, is the culmination of a long period of personal selling experience. It contains three decades worth of insights, strategies, and principles that came about from my own front-line experience, and it offers principles that I created and mastered as I grew and learned as a salesperson.

You will find here advice on mastering your base of key accounts that I believe no other source provides. I'm quite proud of what follows, and I hope it is helpful to you. I hope you will contact me with your comments and your own personal insights on the ideas that appear between these pages. I want to hear about what worked for you, what you would improve, and what you would like to see in future publications.

Please do stay in touch!

Best wishes,

Stephan Schiffman

New York City

1-800-224-2140

contactus@dei-sales.com

About D.E.I.

Founded in 1979 by Stephan Schiffman, D.E.I. is a global sales training organization recognized as one of the nation's premier sales training companies, delivering skills and management programs for organizations ranging from Fortune 500 companies to start-ups.

Using face-to-face training and distance learning programs, we help organizations do what they do better by effecting measurable improvements in the most critical aspects of the sales process:

- prospecting

- execution of the sales process (face-to-face and telephone)

- management of prospecting and selling activity

To date, we have trained more than 750,000 salespeople in North America, South America, Europe, and Asia at more than 9,000 companies, including Nextel Communications, Boise Office Solutions, Cox Communications, Fleet Bank, and Datamonitor, to name a few.

To learn more about our face-to-face training programs, our distance learning initiatives, or our global network of certified franchisees, see pages 249–252. You can find out about franchise opportunities with D.E.I. by contacting:

D.E.I. Franchise Systems
888 7th Avenue, 9th Floor
New York, NY 10106
1-800-224-2140
www.dei-sales.com

ACKNOWLEDGMENTS

This book is a compilation of concepts and principles developed over a long series of years, and I would be remiss if I neglected to mention the following people, each of whom made important contributions to the material between these two covers. My profound gratitude goes out to: Brandon Toropov, Scott Forman, David Rivera, Alan Koval, Ben Alpert, and my friend Stephen Mueller; Jim Levine, Daniel Greenberg, and Stephanie Kip Rostan at the Levine Greenberg Agency; and Gary Krebs and Shoshanna Grossman at Adams Media. Of course, my deepest gratitude goes out, as always, to Daniele, Jennifer, and Anne.

PROLOGUE:
TAKING THE INITIATIVE

Some years ago, when I was working late at night in my office and the administrative assistant had gone home, I decided to answer a ringing phone. I could have let the call go unanswered, but I chose, for some strange reason, to pick up.

It was a fateful choice.

That call was from a manager who had the responsibility for managing one division of a large multinational company. She told me that she wanted to buy ten copies of my book *Cold Calling Techniques (That Really Work!)*.

I said, "That's interesting, most people just buy one copy of that book. Just out of curiosity, why do you need ten copies of the cold calling book?"

(Notice what I did there—I asked her about what was going on in *her* world. In essence, I was asking her about what had changed. What new situation had resulted in her decision to buy ten copies of the book?)

It turned out that she was working with dealers and distributors who represented a company, and she wanted to train them in cold-calling.

I made her a deal.

I responded, "Look, I will fly down and *give* you the books for free. However, in exchange, I want to be able to come down and meet with you and your distributors so I can personally listen to what they're doing on their calls. Does that sound like a fair arrangement?"

It did. Eight weeks later, a small-scale training deal emerged. We trained the distributors in appointment making and helped them to improve their cold calling numbers.

Victory!

Did I stop there, with that one training date?

Well, this is a book about expanding the revenue you get from your key accounts, so you probably already know the answer to that question. I didn't simply let that major company drift off into the night, because I knew that it had *hundreds* of distributors. This company had just paid me to train ten of them. What about the rest?

Here's a question. At that point, after we had spent one day training just ten distributors for that company with all the distributors, was that one big company a *customer*?

Yes, it was.

There was, as I've said, the potential for much more business. Was the big company a key account of mine?

Not yet it wasn't. It was only a *potential* key account. My job was to turn it *into* a key account!

We had worked with one tiny corner of this major oil company. At that point it became my job to reach out to everybody who was responsible for distributors in that company.

Here's what I would say to people, "Hey listen, Mary Jones and I were doing this thing with the ten distributors she's responsible for . . . maybe you and I should get together so I can show you what we did and how it improved her numbers. Are you free next Thursday at 2:00 P.M.?"

I called about sixty people and used some variation on what you just read. That resulted in about 35 initial meetings, and of those meetings, I ended up closing maybe twenty accounts within this large company, accounts that the company paid for at least in part. (Sometimes the distributors would pay for a chunk of the training.)

Now was that oil company a key account of mine?

You bet it was!

■ ■ ■

Those twenty or so programs produced something like two hundred "missionaries" who were REALLY excited about spreading the word within that company about the D.E.I. Appointment Making System. And after about a year's worth of work, we created a buzz. Then the company's distributors started reaching out to *us*.

Finally we got the senior-level people within the company to buy in, and we institutionalized the program. We became the preferred sales training supplier throughout the whole company. That huge company became not just a key account, but a significant piece of ongoing business for us.

So at that point, I asked myself the question—should I stop there?

Well, this is a book about selling, so you know the answer to that question too. What was stopping us from calling other companies in the same industry and setting up pilot programs for them? I couldn't (and didn't) compromise any confidential information we'd gathered about the first company. Instead, I could (and did) ask people at other companies if we could set up free pilot programs with a select group of *their* distributors, with the understanding that, if the free programs went well, they'd consider reimbursing their distributors for a portion of the training costs when the program rolled out on a larger level.

Well, that is exactly what we did.

Now, before I had actually sold any programs to one of those companies, were they, technically speaking, customers of mine?

Nope. When I was delivering free training programs to a handpicked group of distributors, I wasn't dealing with customers. *Yet*. But, they were potential key accounts, because they matched the profile of one of my existing key accounts.

I eventually convinced two more large companies in the same industry to buy training from us for their distributors. And when that happened, those oil companies also became key accounts for my company. We've repeated the pattern in a number of other industries since then.

To this day, I am glad I picked up that phone instead of letting it go to voice mail. We might have simply taken the order for the ten books!

■ ■ ■

Let me tell you another story about a chemical company we worked with. One salesperson at this chemical company told me his "Number one major account" was a company I'll call Massive Lubricants. This lubricant company used my client's chemicals.

Then, I asked this salesperson, "How many people at Massive are there who could conceivably choose to buy the chemicals you sell?"

He stopped and thought for a moment, and then he said, "Probably about 400."

Then I asked, "How many contacts do you have at Massive Lubricants?"

He said, "Two."

I said, "When was the last time you picked up the phone and shared a brand-new idea with one of those two people?"

He shook his head and said, "I can't really remember the last time I did that."

I said, "Guess what? It's time for you to become the idea guy!"

He said, "What do you mean?"

I said, "You've got to get on the phone to your two contacts and start sharing ideas about different ways their company could be using your chemicals. There is a vast, undertapped market within this account, and you're not doing anything about it. At the very least, you've got to get on the radar screen of the two people you do know and start sharing some brainstorms about other places people could start using your products. That's the only way you're really going to generate any internal buzz or build up a referral base."

He started making a point of taking each of his contacts out to lunch—for the express purpose of discussing new ideas about different applications that could connect at different portions of Massive Lubricants. He started generating internal referrals. His contact base exploded. And he grew that account.

■ ■ ■

Both of those examples demonstrate a willingness to take the initiative and to make something new happen within the account. Both of them implement a selling philosophy based on taking the initiative and stirring things up—intelligently. It's that philosophy that I want to share with you in this book.

PART

THE BASICS

SOME DEFINITIONS

When I told the people in our New York office that I was planning to write a book called *Mastering Your Key Accounts*, I got a lot of different reactions from people about the content they expected.

I was intrigued by the variations in the responses, and so I tried to come to terms with what could account for it. I decided that part of the reason that the title of this book could provoke so many different reactions had to do with the usage of the term *key account*. This phrase actually means different things to different people.

I decided to try to clarify matters by opening the book with a discussion of the key distinctions of the key terms that I will be using here.

A *key account* is an account that you can count on for repeat business over time. That is it. So the multinational oil company that posted a profit of $36 billion last year could constitute a key account for you, if you sell a product or provide a service on an ongoing basis to people who work in that organization. By the same token, the homegrown business that your next-door neighbor operates could also be a key account, if, that is, what you are selling is of use to him on an ongoing basis. Of course, the strategies for maximizing your business with the huge multinational company are going to be a little different than the strategies that you will use to win repeat business from your one-person show. But, in my world, they can both count as key accounts, because the sale repeats and has the potential to grow over time. Improving the relationship and the selling skills in such a way that it *does* grow over time, is what this book is all about.

The term *primary contact* refers to either your first and/or most important decision maker within that multinational oil company or to the next-door neighbor who buys from you on a regular basis. Basically, I am using this term to describe your point of entry into the decision-making process. It is possible that you might change your primary contact, and given the turnover at some of the companies you sell to, it is likely.

An *influencer* is someone who may not actually have the final authority to purchase your products and services, but one who can and does exercise considerable sway over that decision. Obviously, it is a good idea to have some kind of relationship with the influences in your sales cycle. It could be the wife of your next-door neighbor who will determine whether he buys from you or it could be a large group of people in purchasing, human resources, or procurement who may play a similar role in a larger organization. Of course, influencers come in all shapes and sizes.

The *decision maker* is the person who makes the final choice to buy from you, or who could get that choice made on your behalf. It is worth noting here that the decision maker is not necessarily your primary contact, although it is certainly possible it could be the same person.

The term *major account* refers to an account that could buy a significant quantity from you, and this type of account definitely has more than one decision maker. (In other words, there's more than one person with the authority to decide to buy from you, or get the decision made on your behalf.) Typically, these are accounts in which one decision maker operates in an entirely different sphere of the business than another one does. A major account can be several smaller companies operating in a way that resembles a single company. We are usually well-advised to treat each decision maker's domain within the major account as a separate world.

RETENTION **101:** THE RIGHT STRATEGY FOR HOLDING ON TO YOUR BUSINESS

Sometimes, during press interviews, I'll hear people ask me to summarize, in a single sentence, something about sales. Usually, what they're asking about is impossible to condense into just a few words.

For instance, they'll say, "We have thirty seconds left before we have to go to commercial—tell our listeners how to make the perfect prospecting call."

Guess what? You can't do it in thirty seconds.

Or they'll say, "In ten words or less, tell our viewers how to manage their prospect base."

I never know what to say. We can (and do) spend a whole day on the topic, just like we can (and do) spend a whole day on the topic of making the perfect prospecting call. Ten words or thirty seconds just isn't enough.

You know what I keep waiting for? The interviewer who says, "You've only got time for one sentence—what's the best advice you can give salespeople for holding on to key accounts?"

That question I do have a single-sentence answer for. So if you're a broadcaster reading this and strategizing for a future interview with me, I encourage you to ask me to provide that answer. Here's what you'll hear in response.

"Don't give your competition any ammunition."

I'm not kidding. If you just follow that advice, you really will hold on to your most important key account relationships.

And then, if the interviewer said to me, "That's fascinating. The president of the network just gave me five more minutes, can you elaborate on that for us?" this is what I'd say:

> "When we train salespeople, we tell them to *not* ask questions like 'What keeps you up at night about your current vendor?' or 'What would you change about your provider?' when they're talking to a new customer. Instead, we tell them to focus on what the prospect is doing, and then follow up on those questions. That's just a much higher-information sales philosophy. It uncovers more. But once you uncover the right information and close the deal, you have to take into account the possibility that *your competitors* might ask those kinds of questions, and you have to beat them to the punch. You should have regular meetings with all of your key accounts and pose those very same questions about *your own company*. You have to be brave enough to ask your own customer, 'Is there anything about what we're doing that keeps you up at night?' You have to be brave enough to ask your own customer, 'Is there anything about our relationship that you would change?' Then, here's the hard part, you then have to *stop talking* and listen to what the customer actually says in response, and make a commitment to remedy any problem that the competition might uncover through this line of questioning. If you do this, you'll remove all of the 'ammunition' your competition could discover, and you will in fact do a better job of protecting the key account."

Of course, this ties into customer service, and that's the subject of our next chapter. But before you move on, consider this question:

If eighty percent of a company's business comes from twenty percent of its customer base . . .

. . . how come so many salespeople do absolutely nothing to keep that twenty percent from going to the competition?

THE SALES PROCESS FROM TWO VIEWPOINTS

Why do customers leave? Typically, the answer has something to do with the point at which our indifference to them becomes impossible to ignore. Often, we hear this indifference described as "poor customer service," with the implication that a "good" relationship with the Customer Service Department would solve the problem. I'm not entirely convinced that the better place to look for a solution is the salesperson who closed the sale and has the responsibility for securing additional business from the account.

Consider the following: A seller's level of interest in a sale (and in the decision maker who can make it happen) is frequently greatest near the beginning of the process, when he or she is trying to turn a prospect into a client. For the decision maker, on the other hand, the level of interest is greatest at the end, when the potential sale becomes a reality.

In other words, the salesperson's interest in the relationship often declines at the same point the decision maker's interest is increasing.

Here's my point. Good customer service is, in most cases, nothing more or less than the conscious decision to actually execute the plan we put together to sell to the person in the first place.

Whose job is that? One way or another, it's ours! We, the salespeople, have to make sure the company knows what the customer actually expects out of the closed deal and we have to follow through to make sure that expectation is being fulfilled. Again, we have to *avoid giving our competition any ammunition!*

If we fail to do that, how can we expect to win any business in the future from this account?

What is effective customer service?

Ultimately, it's asking key accounts and potential key accounts (not prospects!) questions like this:

- Is there anything about what we're doing that keeps you up at night?

- Is there anything about our relationship with us that you would change?

- Was there anything you were unhappy about in our last program/project/delivery?

We have to ask those questions *after* we close the deal. We have to ask our *own* customers the same questions our competition is likely to ask. That's what effective customer service really boils down to.

"SO WHAT ARE YOU SAYING?"

I'm suggesting that some people leave because salespeople have demonstrated to them that we have no interest in getting them to stay. I'm saying you can't expect to have ongoing business from any account that you don't meet with periodically (at least once a year, preferably once a quarter) to ask "How are we doing? Did we jeopardize our relationship? What would you change about this relationship?"

Here are some of the excuses salespeople have given me for why they can't possibly/couldn't imagine ever/wouldn't dream of scheduling a meeting with a key contact at a key account for the express purpose of asking the kinds of questions I'm suggesting:

Who has the time? How much time would the quarterly meeting actually take out of your schedule? How much time would you spend trying to win this account back if the competition got it?

I'm not comfortable doing that. The tech people have to answer the questions about rollout and implementation. If there was, in fact, a huge problem that affected the tech people, and it was in danger of costing you *all* your future commissions from this account, would you rather (a) know about it or (b) not know about it? If you answered (*a*), as any salesperson eager to retain a commission should, why on earth would you want to postpone hearing about the problem before it became a crisis?

Don't make waves. This basically translates as, "Don't disrupt my routine." If taking a rote approach to client service costs you tens or hundreds of thousands of dollars in commissions, is it worth disrupting the routine?

Take the plunge. Schedule the meetings. Ask the questions you know your competition will be asking. Listen to the answers. Follow through on them. Get back in touch with your contact and say what you're doing to fix the problem. After all, your attitude toward identifying and resolving your key account's problems will determine the amount of money you make from that account.

So, you've just heard the excuses. What are the *real* reasons we don't stay in contact with our key accounts? I have some ideas.

Let's look again at the question I posed a little earlier:

If 80 percent of your business comes from 20 percent of your customer base, how come so many salespeople do nothing to keep that 20 percent from going to the competition?

Let me try to answer. I think, above and beyond the issues I've already addressed, there are a number of reasons we do not do everything we should to hold on to business that we have worked very, very hard to earn. Let's look at three of them now, as well as some possible remedies for the complacency.

We grow too comfortable with a single person. Any time we imagine that a relationship with one contact will retain the account, we are fooling ourselves. We really do have to make an effort to learn more about the account, and find out who within the account our own contact is dealing and interacting with, reporting to, asking for raises, and so forth. This is just as true for huge accounts like major energy suppliers as it is for a small network of regional retail outlets. If there is more than one person in the organization, it behooves us to know how those people are interacting with each other and who is going to be doing what over the next twelve months. (Another of the reasons it is important for us to know this, of course, is if there is frequently turnover within these organizations, and our main contact is very likely to land someplace else. True, this person could be a point of entry for another piece of business at another organization, but it certainly would be nice to hold onto the key account that we developed!)

We grow complacent. As we have seen, we are very interested in the sale while we are first building it and establishing the relationship but we may become *less* interested in it as the relationship grows and matures. This is a bit of a paradox because most of the profit for the company depends on an ongoing series of commitments and growth within the account. Yet salespeople often view themselves as hunters first and farmers second—regardless of what the job description actually says. Salespeople who view themselves as hunters and who overlook the job of expanding their knowledge and interest in the account over time are the ones who are least likely to benefit from all the work that went into getting the account in the first place.

We don't keep up with changes in the marketplace. Things often move so quickly in the business and technology world that we can often feel a little bit intimidated. It takes work to keep up with changes in the customers' world. The only real way to accomplish this is to become something of a generalist and to be willing to ask with genuine interest what kinds of changes you see on the horizon. We have to find a way to get our minds around the information we learn and how to share that with our technical people who can stay on top of the situations that customers face.

EIGHT COMMON MISCONCEPTIONS ABOUT KEY ACCOUNTS

Here are the eight most common misconceptions about selling to accounts who buy from you over time:

Misconception #1: To get accounts to buy in the first place, you have to be ready to discount heavily. Actually, the key account relationship is usually based on respect for the value of both sides. The repeat purchase often takes place, not because we have discounted everything to the bone, but because we have decided to stand our ground and identify exactly what the real value of the program or product is over time.

Misconception #2: Key accounts take a long time to close. Our experience is that key accounts make decisions to buy from us in about the same sales cycle as accounts that are brand new. That does not mean that you never come across a key account that takes a longer or shorter period of time. It does mean that the averages tend to combine to match your average selling cycle. So, for example, if twenty-five percent of your account base is key accounts who represent repeat business, and seventy-five percent is brand-new customers, we are going to find that the sales process for acquiring new purchase commitments from both groups are going to be comparable.

Misconception #3: There are always multiple decision makers behind any decision to buy. As we will see a little bit later in this book, we have to think about some of the larger key accounts as companies within companies. That means that sometimes there will be individuals even within a very large organization who have full authority to work with us and give us additional business.

Misconception #4: If there is no budget, there is, by definition, no sale. Part of the beauty of talking to people at the higher tiers of some organizations is they can sometimes make the budget when previously there was no such budget. We will talk about that process as well as the process of selling to those top tier individuals later in this book.

Misconception #5: You have to be a known name or have extensive experience within the customer's industry to build repeat business. Actually, you simply have to be attuned to what the prospective customer is trying to accomplish. Many accounts that turned into key accounts for us began *without* a referral as a result of a cold call where we simply matched up our capabilities with what the prospect was trying to accomplish. Some happened because of incidental contact with key people who had never done business with us before.

Misconception #6: You always have to start with the decision maker at the highest level. There are times when it makes perfect sense to reach out to the very top people in an organization. There are also times when that will not be an option for you. Rather than relying on one system as the guiding principle for all of your key account sales, I am going to encourage you to master a variety of strategies to find a point of entry in the account.

Misconception #7: You always have to start at headquarters. No. Sometimes the headquarters location is so far removed from the authority, decision-making precedent, and management know-how that the people at the top of the heap have wisely distanced themselves from the purchasing and deployment of your product and service. In those kinds of situations, spending most of your time at headquarters, or even starting your discussions there, can be a total waste of time.

Misconception #8: Fill in the blank. My experience is that virtually every salesperson who has the duty of selling to key accounts has developed some individualized, inaccurate preconception about the job, some myth or difficulty that is unique to his or her market situation. For instance, when we trained a news retrieval source used by stockbrokers and bond traders, the salespeople we trained were under the impression that the people operating their key accounts were too busy to meet with them in person. The exact opposite turned out to be the case. The people who were using the service sometimes needed on-site help in configuring the network feeds and setting up the computer systems so that the data was displayed in an easy-to-use format. During these face-to-face meetings, salespeople found that they secured several internal referrals and expanded the account even further. That is just one example of a misconception that is specific to a particular selling environment. I am leaving this last category of misconceptions open because it is likely that people in your company have a similar example of received wisdom that may actually be hindering your efforts to expand your key accounts.

NEGOTIATION WITH KEY ACCOUNTS: TEN CORE PRINCIPLES

Here are the ten core principles for successful negotiating during discussions with key accounts.

Principle #1: Ask yourself: When do I walk away? If it's a negotiation, that means you have to be willing to say, at some point, "No deal." The simple fact that there's repeat business in this account does not relieve you of the responsibility for determining where that point is, how you'll deliver the message, and what strategies you can use to uncover different sources of revenue. How strong is your negotiating position? In the final analysis, you can only negotiate from a position of strength if you really *could* walk away. The prospect or client would prefer that you didn't walk away. For every negotiating discussion, try to identify your best alternative to a negotiated agreement.

Principle #2: Know when to delay. The bigger the deal, the more delay there needs to be between the original offer and the negotiated offer. On important deals, consider letting twenty-four hours elapse between offer and counteroffer.

Principle #3: Avoid negotiating against yourself. Negotiating against yourself means counteroffering before you've received a meaningful response from your negotiating partner.

Principle #4: Be prepared to name and defend your price. As salespeople, we must be ready to make the first move and name our opening price, rather than expecting the potential buyer to outline his or her budget for us. But that's not enough. We must also be prepared to explain our price structure so that it is not perceived as an arbitrary figure. We must be prepared to answer these questions: What are the elements that go into the pricing? Why is it a fair price? What benefit does it represent that only we can deliver to the customer?

Principle #5: Never offer to discount. Discounting early means skipping essential steps in the negotiating model. It's easy to discount, but it's a poor negotiating strategy to offer a price concession that no one has asked for. If your negotiation efforts are not built around interests like long-term profitability or sustained market success, or if your low price does not gain you access to future high-volume deals, consider walking away from the negotiations.

Principle #6: Negotiate terms before you negotiate price. Offer to change payment terms before you agree to reduce your price.

Principle #7: Don't give up something for nothing. Even a small concession should result in a parallel concession from the other side.

Principle #8: Don't get hung up on ROI (Return on Investment). Don't waste too much time and energy trying to show exactly how your product or service will pay for itself in a certain number of months. Instead, focus on the measurable benefits of what you offer and how your organization will support the buying organization over time, as part of a long-term partnership.

Principle #9: Help the individual look good. Consider not only the organizational interests, but also the personal interests of your negotiating partner. What is this person's relationship to his boss, staff, or other constituents? What does he wish to change in terms of power, status, personal goals, or career goals? Is he out to prove something to someone? If so, what?

Principle #10: Never change the price without changing the deal. When pressured to reduce your price, do so only after making some kind of alteration in your plan. Ask yourself: If I must change the price, how, specifically, would I reorganize the deal? What is the lowest dollar figure I would accept before walking away?

7

THE INFORMATION GAP

Most of the people we train to master their key accounts start out the training with a major information gap about their customers.

Who is your #1 prospect for repeat business right now?
Please think of the name of the company you consider to be the most important prospect for ongoing business within your universe of key accounts. Please write the name of that company, and the name of your primary contact there, on the lines below.

_____

_____

Now that you've identified this company and the primary contact, please answer the following questions in the spaces provided.

1. When is the next time that you are going back to meet face-to-face with this person? (Please write down *either* the scheduled

date and time for the meeting *or* the words No Next Step in place. Do not enter anything else for this answer.)

_____

2. What does the company do, and who are its customers? (Please write at least three detailed sentences.)

_____

_____

_____

_____

_____

_____

_____

3. How long has your contact been at this company? What was this person doing before this job?

_____

_____

4. Who else are you talking to there *besides* your primary contact? Why?

_____

_____

5. Who are the primary influencers within the account?

_____

_____

6. How much is the account worth to your company over the next twenty-four months?

_____

7. From your perspective, what is the very next thing that has to happen for you to eventually close the next piece of business from this company?

_____

_____

_____

8. When and how will you make that happen?

_____

_____

_____

9. How much total spending is the company doing in areas where we could add value?

_____

_____

10. How much of that spending is going to you?

_____

11. How much of that spending is going to a competitor?

_____

12. Which competitors, specifically, and why them?

_____

_____

_____

_____

13. Is your primary contact the decision maker on the next piece of business? What does the contact think is going to happen next with regard to that piece of business?

_____

_____

14. When is that going to happen?

_____

15. Does the contact want that deal to happen as much as you do?

_____

When we ask people in our workshops to answer these kinds of questions about their #1 key account, it's a bit of a wake-up call. They do not really have great answers for all these questions. In fact, they usually do not have *any* answers for most of these questions, which are, let's face it, pretty basic. If you plan to develop ongoing business from this account, and you know nothing about your primary contact's career history, and have no Next Step in place to discuss what should happen next, then that's not much of a #1 account, in my opinion.

If you had any problems giving detailed answers to the questions you just read—and certainly if you left all the information blank—you probably are at a selling disadvantage because of an information gap. You are deeply vulnerable to the competition. This company may not even be a prospect in the formal sense of the word, even though he or she has bought from you in the past, and may buy from you again at some point in the future!

Our definition for somebody being a prospect requires that we have established some kind of Next Step with them—that they are in fact playing ball with us by slotting out a time on their calendar. (For examples of how to obtain Next Steps with your key accounts, see Appendix B.) Typically, when we're dealing with real, live, honest-to-goodness income-producing prospects within our own key accounts, the time frame for our next meeting tends to be something within the next two to four weeks. At this point, if you were in a face-to-face training program with me, and you told me that you *did not* have a meeting scheduled to meet with your primary contact at your key account within the next two to four weeks, I would urge you to think about how closely you are using the definition of prospect to accurately describe the level of the relationship, the actual snapshot of where you are in the sales cycle, in connection with this particular account.

If the person you thought about as being your number one prospect within your basic key account really has not given you a Next Step, and you do not know any of the answers to the other questions we just posed above, it may be time to think about using a tool that helps you get a little bit closer to using accurate guidelines for knowing when you do and don't have that information.

IS IT REALLY A PROSPECT?

What if you had a ranking tool that would help you to understand the information you have (and don't have) in the key account? What if you had something that would help you recognize more "early warning signs" into the relationship, so you could figure out exactly where you were by asking for an appropriate Next Step? What if you could tell at a glance who is playing ball with you and who is not? What if there were some way to avoid the easy habit of being vague about what exactly is going to happen next and when it is going to happen?

The Prospect Management System, which you will encounter later on in this book, makes it easy to accomplish all of these goals, and master your key accounts.

In our training workshops, after I've asked the questions you read in the previous chapter, and reviewed the answers participants have prepared, I'll ask the toughest question of all: Given what you just told me, *why* do you think this account is your number one prospect?

This is a very humbling question, but it's important. It's the sort of question that separates real prospects from imaginary prospects.

The real problem arises when we try to use uncertain or constantly shifting criteria to identify who is a prospect and who is not. During our training programs, we actually hear things like this:

- "A prospect is someone I went out to lunch with eight months ago."

- "A prospect is someone who bought from me at any time during my employment with the company."

- "A prospect is someone who I have a good social relationship with who might buy from me again."

If you've made it this far in the book, you already have a pretty clear idea of who I consider to be a prospect, and you understand why the three statements you just read fail to pass muster.

I want you to change the way you think about your prospects. From this point forward, I am going to challenge you to never use the word *prospect* to describe anybody with whom you've had a vague, uncertain, or nonscheduled kind of status. I am also going to challenge you to not use that word to describe anybody you have any kind of ongoing discussion with who has exceeded your average selling cycle.

When you and I talk about prospects within your key account base, we are talking about people who really are working through the process with you—against a predefined sales cycle. They are in the calendar, and they are working against the average time phase that you sell in. Otherwise, they're not a prospect, and you can't project income from them on your sales reports.

The whole point of this book is to move away from the common, free-floating notion of a key accounts prospect that lacks any consistent criteria. We want to move toward a more measurable and standardized definition of a prospect. Having no criteria means there is nothing you can measure. And that's not exactly a recipe for improvement!

REAL NUMBERS

Over the years, we've worked with many teams that had the responsibility to manage key accounts. To understand what works (and what doesn't) in the key account environment, you have to understand some principles that illustrate what works (and what doesn't) in all different kinds of sales.

When we begin our training programs we start by giving our own numbers, and then we ask people what their numbers are. We feel that if we give our numbers first it is easier for others to tell us about their own activities. Here's how we do that.

I say, "Even though I am the president of the company, an author, and a lecturer, I still sell sales training and speeches. Every day that I'm not in front of a group, I pick up the phone and I dial the phone fifteen times."

Then I draw a big fifteen on the flip chart.

15

Sometimes I will stop there when I am delivering this program and I will say to one of the training participants, "How many times a day do you dial the phone to generate new business?"

I'll do this just to get them to feel a little more interactive and to establish that, even though their numbers are not going to be my numbers, there is still a parallel between what I am talking about and what they do.

I then say, "As a result of making fifteen calls I will speak to seven people. We use the expression *completed call* to describe what happens in those seven conversations."

15 : 7

"That means," I continue, "that I speak to the person I want to speak to, the person who *could* set up an appointment with me to meet and talk about sales training with our company.

"As a result of speaking to those seven people I will set up one new First Appointment. I do that on average five days a week, so that I end up with five new First Appointments. I end up with eight total visits a week, combined with my continuing visits, as a result.

15 : 7 : 1
8

"Now let me just explain something. The difference between an appointment and visit is this. If I pick up the phone and ask somebody to meet with me next Tuesday at 3:00, and they agree to do that, I have set an appointment. But every time I actually walk in the door of a place to talk about doing a piece of business with someone, I am going on a visit. The visit is not necessarily the appointment. The appointments I set will eventually become visits."

Then I ask a question: "So, why eight rather than five? Or ten?"

People usually struggle with that for a couple of minutes, and eventually I explain the answer like this: "Well, as a result of making eight appointments, what happens? You will go on some of the appointments. Of course, sometimes when you show up the contact is not there. Sometimes the contact is there and it never goes beyond that first meeting, and sometimes you go and as a result of that meeting there is another meeting and another meeting after that! So there are eight visits on the average week, which are a combination of first visits and continuing visits.

"Now, my numbers are that for every eight visits I go on, I get one sale, which I do on average fifty weeks a year. In the end, I have fifty new pieces of business and those fifty sales provide a lifestyle.

$$15 : 7 : 1$$
$$8 : 1$$
$$50$$

10 THE CHALLENGE

Then comes the challenge. At this point, I pick out someone from the group and say, "Let me ask you about your activity. I'm just curious, how many appointments do you go on in an average week?" And whatever that number is, I am going to ask, "Why that number?"

Sometimes I ask about that number, and even before they can formulate an answer I will stop them and say, "Please notice that I am not saying that your number is good or bad. I am not putting any value judgment on it at all. I just want to know why, if it is two visits a week, why is it two? Why not three? Why not one? "

People who don't focus on generating much of their revenue from key accounts will typically give me answers like this:

- "The reason I make the number I make is that I don't have enough leads."

- "That's all the time I have."

- "My boss told me to do it that way."

They give a variety of reasons. Sometimes I will ask, "Did your boss say you could not do any more than that number?" Then I turn to the flipchart, which now has this on it:

$$15:7:1$$
$$8:1$$
$$50$$

Then, I will say, "Notice that I make five first new appointments every week. Why is that? Why do you think I do that?"

The same question I just asked about them, I'm asking about myself, "Why do I do that?"

Typically, the participants of the program will try to attach *their* reasons to what my motivation is for setting those appointments. They might say, "To fill up your week," for instance. So this is the point in the program where I will explain that no, the real reason I make five appointments each week is not to fill up the week, and not because five is a magical number. I set five new appointments each week because doing so gives me the results that I need in order for me to be successful—specifically, the fifty sales a year.

"In other words," I say, "you also could have said that the reason you do what you do every week is so that you can hit your annual income goal. But that's not what you said. In a sense, there was a disconnect between the activity and your goals." And helping salespeople to overcome that disconnect is what my whole career has really been all about.

This book will help you make sure there is an absolute connection between your activity—whatever it is—and your goals. It does not matter to me if you need two, six, or sixteen meetings a week. The point is that whatever number you need should be based on relationships between your various activities, and on something that you want to make happen at the end of that week. There is no one right number for everybody, but there does have to be an absolute connection between talking to people and making a sale.

More important, we have to understand that whether we know our ratios, we do in fact have ratios, no matter what kind of field we sell in, no matter how complex our sale is, or how simple our sale is. There are ratios that affect what our income eventually turns out to be for that year.

11 WHAT WORKS

If you think about it, *everybody* knows how to sell *something*. It's just a question of how efficiently. After all, everybody who tries to sell something—even a brand-new hire who knows virtually nothing about your industry—will eventually sell something. The real challenge lies in the fact that what we "eventually" sell is not enough!

Frequently, not only do the goals go up, but the time that we have available to attain those goals stays the same, or actually *decreases*. Why? Any number of reasons. Maybe you have new responsibilities in servicing new accounts, maybe the territory changes, or maybe the competition becomes more intense. One way or another, the challenge of selling is in continuously improving. How could you improve with less actual selling time to improve?

Let me challenge you to look at that question in another way. What specific ways are there for us to monitor our improvement? As it happens, no matter what you sell there are really only five ways that you can improve.

Look at those daily, weekly, and yearly numbers once again:

$$15:7:1$$
$$8:1$$
$$50$$

Usually, but not always, when I ask people how they could improve this performance, the first strategy for improvement that they offer has to do with the "dials". So, I will circle the number *15*, which is the number of dials each day.

Yes, you could conceivably increase your dials. I might also suggest that I could look at other ways to support my decision to try to make more dials, like managing my time better. In the end, though, what I am really looking at is something related to ratios connected to the number of dials that I make every day. If I were able to double my dials, and keep all the other ratios the same, my numbers would go up.

In theory, sales is a numbers game. In theory, we could all add more dials and if we did that arithmetically and kept all the other ratios the same, then yes, we would in fact make more money.

The reality is that we cannot always make more dials.

So what else could we do? While keeping the dials at least at the level they are, I mean.

As it turns out, there are four other things that we could do. One is a ratio improvement between dials and completed calls.

Consider this: I could make more money simply by improving my dial to completed call ratio without adding more dials. Instead of fifteen dials leading to seven completed calls, I could make that fifteen dials leading to *eight* completed calls. And if all the other ratios stayed the same, my income would increase.

Another thing I can do, of course, is get more of my completed calls to become appointments. Instead of the ratio being 7:1, suppose I worked on improving my skills and made it 7:2. All of a sudden, I just made more money.

Now, if I can get from 7:1 to 7:2 just by changing what I was doing on the phone, would you say that that new technique works? And of course, the answer is yes.

7 : 1 >> 7 : 2 = "WORKS"!

Do you see what we just did? We have defined what works. People are always asking sales trainers, "Does it work when you do X?" or "Does it work when you do Y?" and "Don't you think it would work better if I did Z?"

The real answer to "Does it work?" is this: "When you do it, do your ratios improve?"

Not "Do I like doing it that way better?" and certainly not, "If I was a customer, I would prefer it if a salesperson did that." Instead, we are going to define the idea of something "working" as something very tangible and very specific, namely, something that improves one of these ratios.

It is not that any technique will work 100 percent of the time and never fail. It is not that you are never going to reach somebody who would prefer not to hear from a salesperson at that moment. And we cannot say that because we once had an argument with someone, or that somebody once got upset, that that technique does not work. What works is what you do that results in your ratios improving.

Another area I could focus on is I could get more of my visits to become sales. Instead of eight visits leading to one sale, for example, let's say that each eight visits leads to *two* sales.

As it turns out, that is a whole different skill set. Getting my visits to turn into sales is all about selling skills and strategizing, and to some degree, even *minimizing* the number of visits I make to people who would eventually *not* buy, so I could spend more time with people who *will* buy.

Another thing I could do is get more of my sales that I finally do get just to be bigger. That is, I could sell a greater average value. I could sell more profitably. I could penetrate the account more effectively. I could sell two things instead of one on average, and make my average sale bigger. If my average sale doubles and everything else stays the same, that is another way I could make more money without changing anything else. Again, that would be a classic example of something actually "working" in a way that really is meaningful and measurable.

■ ■ ■

Your current ratios are based on your current habits. If you keep doing what you're doing right now, yes, you are going to continue to sell, but you are also going to continue to have the same ratios and you will not improve.

So I am going to challenge you at various points in this book to do things in a different way with your key accounts than you may be doing with them right now. That's not because your way of doing something is "wrong," and not because what you're doing doesn't "work," but because I want you to try other ways. That is my job—to challenge you and show you ways you could improve. Your job is not necessarily to buy into everything you read in this book. What you might want to do is as we go along, keep a written list of all the things I suggest that are a little different than the way you're selling right now. Once you finish the book, select a few things that you commit to try. See if they work better than what you're doing.

Remember, *works* means it helps you improve your ratios measurably, even to a small degree. Remember, selling is all about improving over time.

12

WHAT ALL THIS HAS TO DO WITH YOU

Ratios really do matter when it comes to key account selling, and these foundation principles you've just been reading about really do connect to the quality of your relationships with account primary contacts, influencers, and decision makers. Let me take a moment to explain how and why that is.

When I ask key accounts people whether their income targets are higher this year than they were last year, they always say yes. When I ask key accounts people whether the amount of time that they have available to work their key accounts this year is greater or smaller, they always say smaller.

How are we going to bridge that gap?

You can't just say, "Well, I'm going to work harder this year," because that implies that, up to this point, you were holding back somehow. With people who have the responsibility to grow the income from their key accounts, that's usually just not the case. Most of the time, they're already going flat out.

And you can't really say, "I'm going to work smarter," either. At least, I don't think *smarter* is the right word, because that implies that there was a level of hidden ignorance in play before you got this year's quota, and I don't think that's the case.

Whenever anybody tries to tell me that they plan to "work harder" or "work smarter" in a key account context, here's my question: "What ratio is going to get better as a result of your working harder or working smarter?" In other words, we aren't going to try to use some kind of vague terminology that sounds soft or fuzzy or fundamentally unmeasurable and then try to implement that. Instead, we're going to identify a particular strategy or technique as either being effective or ineffective. *Effective* means it improves one of these activity ratios we're keeping an eye on. *Ineffective* means it doesn't improve one of those activity ratios. It's as simple as that.

What I think people are trying to get at when they say "I want to work smarter on my key accounts," is: They want to work *more efficiently* on their key accounts. I absolutely agree.

I am going to propose to you that you want to understand and implement some of the skills that I share with somebody who is, technically, a "non–key account" salesperson. Specifically, you want to find out how to make calls more efficiently within what may be a limited prospect base, how to gather information more efficiently, and how to get more efficient at setting face-to-face meetings with those people. That last element has huge philosophical implications, by the way, because all the ratios we're talking about are built around the idea of securing a Next Step: a spot on the other person's calendar. If we get more efficient with that, if we become more accomplished at actually measuring how often that happens, then we really are going to see measurable improvements.

You also have those same five potential ways to improve. However, it's possible that you have far fewer leads than a salesperson who is not entrusted with growing a key account. Many of the salespeople I work with simply can't "add more dials" to their day, because they are working with a very limited number of potential buyers. But, if they could find a few more dials *within each account*, and kept that up over the weeks and months, they could make a measurable difference!

Unlike most salespeople, you may have a limited ability to simply move on to a whole new company. That means you have to get *quite good* at the following:

- Turning the completed calls you make within your key accounts into meetings to discuss new pieces of business. (These calls can be "cold," or they can be based on referrals.)

- Converting visits into sales. (This means gathering the right information and developing the right Next Step strategy and building the right proposal.)

- Increasing the average value of what you sell. (This means positioning yourself in front of the right top-level person in the account and saying, "I think I can deliver X benefit, *if* you let me talk to the following twelve people, and *if* you let me report back to you at this date and time. At that time I can tell you all about what I find out and how we might be able to implement this." Statistically speaking, you're going to find that dealing with real decision makers in this way will result in higher value deals.)

The best account managers succeed year after year by mastering the basic skills, not ignoring them. In the pages that follow, I want to show you the best strategies we've come up with for doing just that.

THE SALES MODEL

13

Let's start by looking at selling from the back of the process and think about what has to happen before the purchase decision happens. Once you start thinking about it that way, the whole process becomes more logical.

Look at the decision to buy. It's the last part of the sales process, and it obviously corresponds with the salesperson's job description, to *close the sale*. After all, that's the whole reason you're reading this book: to close more sales.

We call it *close* because that's the common terminology for it in most sales management environments. The truth is that because this is a book about repeat business, it's much more likely that we're going to be interested in *opening* the business over time and *expanding* the relationship so that there's more than one purchase decision on a regular basis.

I'm going to keep referring to that decision as the "close," since that's the most popular way that people have come to remember and understand it. What I really want, if I stop to think about it, is for the customer to use my services, use them fully, enjoy using them, and use them forever, at a profit to me and my organization.

I want this customer ultimately to become a key account and to use all my company's services. The good news is they will. They will buy and they will use our products. I will close the deal if, and only if, it makes sense to the customer to do so.

```
┌─────────────┐
│   MAKES     │
│   SENSE     │
└─────────────┘
```

Let's stop here and acknowledge something right now. There are customers in our key account base right now who are doing things in a way that we may find primitive, difficult, or inefficient. It may be that we think they're paying too much and getting too little. To us, what they're doing "doesn't make any sense." Why would they do it that way?

Why would somebody purchase what they're purchasing right now if it doesn't make sense to us for them to do it that way? *The only conceivable reason they do that it that it really does makes sense for them to do so—from* their *perspective.*

Why did they decide to go that way in the first place? What was the thought process? Who were the people involved? Why did they do it that way first? Why haven't they made changes in years? The answers to those questions are something that they understand, *something that makes sense to them.* Not to us—yet.

Therefore, my sale must make sense from their point of view in order for them to purchase whatever it is that I'm selling.

If that's the case—what should our method for closing the sale sound like?

THE RIGHT CLOSING TECHNIQUE

I close the sale by very simply asking one all-important question: "Makes sense to me, what do you think?"

Look at it again. When I ask that question, I'm going to get an answer, but I'm not trying to manipulate an answer.

I'm hoping that they'll say yes. And of course if they say yes, I will close the sale. But I'm not trying to trick them into saying yes. I'm only learning what's already on their mind. So I say, "Hey, this makes sense to me, what do you think?" They're either going to say yes it does make sense to them too, or no, it doesn't make sense. And if they say no, that's okay, because I'm always ready for that response. If they say no, then at that stage I can step back and say, "Really? I'm just curious, why doesn't it make sense to you? Why wouldn't you want to go ahead?" Then I've got a discussion I can work with. I'm going to hear why it doesn't make sense to them, and by extension I'll then know what does make sense.

So the close, relative to the other steps of the selling process, is really the shortest and simplest step of all. But the question is how do I get there?

Before I get to the close, I have to present.

PRESENT	CLOSE (Makes sense)

Now the word *present* suggests I'm going to stand in front of you and tell you what's going to make sense, or that I'm going to guess what might make sense. I think a better word might be *plan*, and perhaps the best description of all is the *reason* that it makes sense for somebody to use my product or service. But let's follow convention and call this step that happens right before the close, *presentation*.

In order for you to buy my product or service even for the first time, much less for subsequent times, I've got to give you a reason that really does make sense for you to do so.

Before I present, I have to gather information.

Before I do that, I have to open up the discussion. Some people call this *qualifying*. Whatever you call it, it's the discussion that leads to the information phase. I don't just start hammering away with questions before I establish that connection. So there are really four steps to every sale.

OPEN/ QUALIFY	INFORMATION	PRESENT	CLOSE (Makes sense)

During our training programs, I ask, "If there are four steps in the selling process, what's the objective of the first step?" The right answer is a little surprising to some people: to get to the Next Step!

So we're always moving forward. Where do we want, ideally, to spend most of our time? In the information-gathering step. In fact, we say that 75 percent of our work in the sales process has to come *before* we make a recommendation.

Let me demonstrate the importance of this principle to you now. Do you see this dot?

•

That single dot is *one* of the reasons I might have articulated in order to get a customer of mine to decide that it does in fact make sense to buy more from me. That is one of the ways I could have bundled up my product and services. That dot is one of the many options, one of the ways I could have presented my sale.

Now, this dot over here,

•

is another way I could have priced it.

Here is a different way I could have structured my proposal.

•

And here's a different point at which I could have entered the account.

•

In fact, look how many dots, proposals, plans, or potential solutions I could conceivably have delivered to my prospects!

Every one of these dots is another way it could have gone. And how many of those dots could I identify? Well, in theory, an infinite number. Which is the only one that I really want to show? What I really want to present is this one right here:

That one dot with the arrow next to it is the plan, the reason that makes sense to the other person. That is the one that, after I present it and I ask, "It makes sense to me, what do you think?" The customer says, "Yeah, you know what? It really does make sense to me." That is the dot they are going to say yes to, because it really does make the most possible sense from my buyer's point of view.

How do I figure out which is the right dot? By asking the right questions in the information phase! That's why we want to spend most of our time in that second step of the selling process. In fact, we've even got a substep—after we think we've gathered and checked the information, we're going to verify the information we've accumulated. Ideally, we're going to do that verification work before we present to any potential customer.

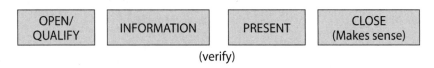

(verify)

Now, consider that dot that represents the plan that makes the most possible sense to my prospect. Is that the only dot I could have presented? Of course not. There are plenty of other dots that I could have presented. Sometimes, in fact, if I present one of those dots, it will in fact produce a sale, even if the sale doesn't make the most possible sense to the other person, and even if the information I'm working with has been imperfectly verified. Do you want to know why? Because of the *Rule of One-Third*.

This is how it works: One-third of the time the salesperson presents the wrong package, develops the wrong offer, talks to the wrong person, about the wrong price, at the wrong time, *and still gets that sale*. Why? Because a third of the time we are going to get the sale anyway.

A third of the time we showed up at the right time, they were ready, they were ready to switch, and for whatever reason we get sales. You and I both get those sales. The sale more or less falls into our laps. I call these sales the "first-third" sales. (I cannot really help you get more of those.)

Let's look at the next third. Those sales, even if you do show the right plan, the right recommendation, the right proposal, the right pricing, the right timing, and you are talking to the right person, you are not going to get the sale. Do you know why you are not going to get the sale? The other salesperson showed up first.

And who is the other salesperson?

Actually, the other salesperson is your competition. And here's the big question: *Who is your biggest competition?*

15 THE COMPETITION

Who is your biggest competition? As it turns out, your biggest competition is not any individual company, although, I get plenty of people giving the names of particular companies when I ask them who the biggest competitor is. Actually, your biggest competition is the **status quo**. I wouldn't shout this if I could. You are always selling against what they are doing now.

Maintaining the status quo is what your potential clients are doing right now. The reason it makes sense to them right now, whatever it is, is the status quo. Think about it. Whatever they are doing now, they are doing right now because it makes sense to keep doing it. People who decide not to change what they're doing (by buying from you) do so because whatever they are doing now works.

Maybe the status quo is not the greatest thing, maybe they're not superhappy, but the status quo works well enough to keep. It makes sense. It's interesting to note that there are quite a few studies out there that suggest that the number one reason people do not change a business decision is a lack of reassurance.

The number two reason is the fear of change.

Yes, there is a risk in changing anything. Let's face it. If I champion some big new initiative, even from a vendor I've worked with before, and

I bring a new way of doing something into my company and *anything* goes wrong at all, there is a political problem for me. It's risky.

On the other hand, there is no risk to doing nothing—there is no risk to *not* changing. (Or at least there is often perceived to be. no risk.)

Here's what we have to come to terms with: People buy with their emotions and later rationalize that decision. And you know what? The converse is also true. People also choose *not* to buy for emotional reasons. The two biggest reasons we have to overcome are (1) lack of reassurance and (2) fear.

16 "FINAL-THIRD" SALES

Now, I mentioned earlier that there was a third of the time that the sale would come our way, and that there was also a third of the time a sale would not come our way. And there's that final third, where our actions affect the outcome.

In that final third, there are two traits we should take into account.

The people we actually do end up working with from that final third have two key characteristics in common. First, they are continuously moving forward to the Next Step of the sales process with us, and second, they are moving on to the step within our normal timeframe.

For most salespeople, this is a difficult concept. It is easy when you are tracking time for another person's sale and you are looking at that clinically, but it is often difficult to see it when it is your own sale. That is the point. Every sale has a normal amount of time within which that sale happens. If you looked at every sale you have ever closed over the past five years and then you asked when the sale began and when it finally closed, you would come up with an average.

Of course, there would be some deals that exceeded that average, and some that came in well under that average. But isn't that the whole point of the concept "average," that some things are longer and some things are shorter? My point is that there would be a middle ground beyond which most sales do not go.

Yes, some deals do close in an hour. Some sales take months or years. However, what do *most* of them do? Whatever the answer is, that is your sales cycle.

In my industry, the sales cycle is approximately eight weeks. Yes, there are some deals that happen in a day and a half, and there are also some deals that unfold over a period of four or five months. But that is the far end of the bell curve in either direction. Most of our sales, about 80 to 90 percent, unfold within the broad timeline of six to eight weeks. And notice that this happens whether we have done business with the company before or not. So really the fact that we have done business with huge international energy companies, the fact that we did a pilot program with them two months ago, does not necessarily speed up the six to eight weeks. The average with them is maybe nine or ten weeks, but in fact it does not instantly accelerate it. We can be dealing with additional business from a customer of ours, and we are still going to have that average sales cycle to look at and compare with. So what does that mean? It means that any sale that takes longer than eight weeks is not fitting the pattern. Now what would be a reason that a sale would not be fitting the pattern? Assume that it is a sale at a company that we have already done business with. What could conceivably cause that sale to be anomalous, to take longer than eight weeks?

And here's the most important question: Why would I want to assume that a sale that was not fitting the pattern would be likely to happen? After all, if it is not fitting the pattern statistically it is much closer to matching up with the pattern of sales that do not come my way!

Remember: a sale that goes on for longer than its average selling cycle is less likely, not *more* likely, to happen. And that is going to be something important to take into account as we are deciding what we want to invest our energy in.

And so, when I think about all the potential prospects in the course of a year that I could meet with, if I just apply these two simple principles I am already going to have a very clear, compelling case for identifying which people I want to spend my time with. I want to focus on those people who have set up a Next Step that unfolds within my typical average timeline. That automatically eliminates 90 percent of the people that I would be likely to pour vast amounts of time and energy into without getting any payoff.

BREAKING IT DOWN

Let's look at all the business we could conceivably generate from our key accounts in a single year. I'm going to represent that revenue with this image:

BUSINESS

You know what? I need a certain number of prospects—we will call it the X number—to reach that desired number of sales from our base of key accounts. Well, what do I know about that number of potential prospects within my key account base? The one thing I know with certainty is that the number of prospects for new business (X) is going to be *larger* than the number of pieces of total business that I close.

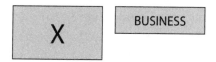

In fact, if I knew my prospect-to-sale ratio I could actually predict how many sales I was going to get from my key accounts by looking at my prospect base!

Think about it. If I needed to change the total sales I was actually going to get, the only way for me to do that would be to change what was happening with my prospect base! I can get the prospects on average to be worth more money and/or I can increase the total number of potential deals that I am talking about, either with brand-new customers or customers that I have done business with in the past.

So where do my prospects come from? Well, before my prospects became prospects, at one point they were simply opportunities. Simply writing a name on a piece of paper or entering a name of a company into a computer database does not move the sales process forward, even though these people may be highly qualified to use or implement what I sell or be greatly benefited from what I have to offer.

The fact that they are good potential candidates for using my product or service does not necessarily mean I have set up any meaningful Next Step yet. Remember: the objective of each step in the sales process is to get to the Next Step!

For them to be prospects, I have to develop a relationship with them—evidence that we're working out something that really could make sense to them. In other words, I must have a Next Step, something that's scheduled in the other person's calendar. And what's more, the sale has to be unfolding within my typical sales cycle.

Let's say I pick up the phone and I call up one of the people who are in that opportunity, or "Not Prospects Yet," group. Suppose that during that call I say, "Would you agree to sit down with me and discuss what we might be able to do together in the year to come?" Then suppose this person agrees to have that discussion with me next Tuesday at 2:00 P.M. At that point, this is no longer simply an opportunity. But it's not a prospect yet because we haven't yet had the meeting. I would suggest that there is yet another group of people to consider as "Not Prospects Yet"—those who have given us a First Appointment to discuss the possibility of doing business with us.

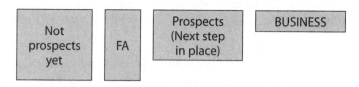

If I picked up the phone and called everyone on my list who fell into that "opportunity" category, some, but not all of them, would agree to have that kind of a meeting or discussion with me. Those who did would qualify as First Appointments, or FAs. I have scheduled a future initial discussion in the other person's datebook, and I know he is setting aside a certain amount of time to talk with me about some new possible way of using my product or service. We have not yet had that conversation, but we've scheduled it.

In fact, those initial discussions actually drive the process of turning opportunities into prospects. It takes a certain number of First Appointments (or initial contacts, if you prefer) to make that total prospect base happen.

That prospect base, the information to the right of the FA column, could actually be divided even further. We can get a little bit more specific with that and assign different ranks, different levels of development, and different labels to each of the active prospects that have gone beyond that scheduled First Appointment. I can call them ones and twos and threes, and insert all of them in place of the third of the four steps of the sales process that we've identified. (Step four, of course, corresponds with the box marked "Business.")

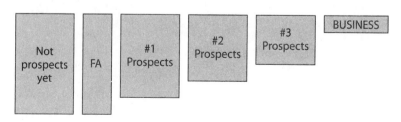

The one thing I do know immediately, even if I do not know any of the criteria that I would assign to the various prospects, is that not every possible deal is going to turn into business for me. In fact, I am going to need a larger number of ones to generate a certain number of twos. I am going to need a larger number of twos to generate a certain number of threes, and my number threes are going to yield a smaller number of closed sales. That's what you see reflected in the diagram above.

Think of it this way. My appointments (A) will give me my prospects (P), and my prospects will give me my sales (S).

$$A > P > S$$

Think about it. We are starting a discussion about a new revenue-generating activity from our organization, a new way they can use what I offer. That big *A* represents the total number of appointments I initially schedule to discuss those new deals. I have to have a huge number of As to turn them into actual live Ps, or prospects. And I must have a large number of prospects that can turn into the total sales that I want in a given period.

In our industry, the sales training industry, we typically find that it takes two First Appointments to generate one actual real, live prospect. And yes, those First Appointments can come from people we have already worked with before.

About 50 percent of them move forward into being live prospects who have set up a Next Step with us and are moving through the process within our timeline. I have to identify the right amount of appointment-making activity to maintain the base of prospects at a certain level, the level that makes sense for our company in terms of our overall income goal.

FOUR P'S

Let's look at the four essential selling activities. They appear only by their first letter in our training workbooks:

P

P

P

P

When I talk to groups that I'm training in key account selling, I make a special point of putting a good deal of emphasis on that first *P*. It stands for *prospecting*. Sometimes that word confuses people whose goal it is to build new business from existing accounts.

What is prospecting for our purposes?

Prospecting within existing accounts means moving on to something new, either something new in this account, with this contact, or something new in some other part of the company. I can prospect within an existing account simply by moving to a new discussion of a different sale or application. Basically, anytime I move on to some new way of increasing the usage of whatever it is I sell, I am prospecting.

We symbolize that activity, prospecting, with that first letter *P*.

The second *P* is *presenting*, which is all about making the right recommendation. I've already talked about how that works—how the presentation should be based on the right *reason* to buy.

Let's look at the third *P*, which is *product knowledge*. That goes beyond simply knowing your product. It connects to the *stories* of how and why people use your product. What types of applications do people have for your product? What made your very best customer decide to work with you in the first place? What about your biggest customer? (Notice that the biggest one-time customer may not be the best customer in terms of long-term repeat business.) For example, if I showed a company how to use my product to do something completely unusual—something that has never been done before but could be done with my product—I am demonstrating product malleability. That really is what we are talking about when we are talking about product knowledge.

Then finally there is the fourth *P, professional development*. That is the fourth key and it means doing things that help develop professional skills—for instance, reading this book. You, right now, are engaged in professional development. Going to a training program would also be an example of that, as would listening to a tape that has some connection to your skills and capacity as a salesperson.

Well, unfortunately, we cannot do all of these all the time. We might wish we could, but the truth of the matter is that we cannot. We cannot spend 100 percent of our time in each area.

At my company, we have closely studied the best salespeople, people who have made more than $100,000 a year in commissions, and by that I mean people who have done so for at least ten years. This is what they have told us. They said that 45 percent of their success has come from the first *P*—prospecting, or moving on. 45 percent! That's a big number. (Understand that we are talking about 45 percent of the time that they spend doing these four things—that is not necessarily 45 percent of the average workday, but simply how they rank these four activities in terms of the contributions to their own success.)

Presenting accounts for 20 percent of their success. Now if you think about it, that actually makes a certain amount of sense. If I am selling in the field, there are only so many hours that I could physically be in front of somebody to make a presentation. If I presented and did nothing else, I would eventually run out of people to present to.

What about the third *P*? The most successful people attribute 20 percent of their success to their product knowledge. That means, in the final analysis, that they know their success stories. By the way, the best salespeople know at least ten and sometimes many more than ten success stories *cold*. These are stories they can instantly incorporate into a discussion about their product or service. They're quite comfortable discussing how and why their best customers actually use the products and services, and you should be too.

Finally, 15 percent of what the best salespeople do is attributed to professional development.

The way I have just laid it out just told you what the answers are. You now know how much emphasis you should be placing on each of these activities, relative to the activities themselves.

These are the four things that everybody who sells key accounts has to do, and has to continue to do, in order to make sales. It is worth noticing that prospecting piece, which we are going to understand as simply moving on when there is no reason to believe that a given initiative is going to fly, is the primary determinant of your success. Your ability to move on, to propose a new idea when an old idea is not being implemented, really is going to be critical in terms of your ability to succeed in the key account.

When I ask people who sell to key accounts to rank these four activities, however, I get some answers that are kind of startling. When I ask them to prioritize the activities, they might attribute 50 percent of their success to product presentation. Whenever I hear somebody say that to me, I always stop them and give them a little reality check. I say, "Okay, fine, how would you allocate the rest of the available time?" After I have established what the right answers are and that they have been proven to have been the right answers by people who have earned a great deal of money over a very long time—I circle the first two elements like this.

- Prospecting: 45%

- Presentation: 20%

- Product knowledge/malleability: 20%

- Professional development: 15%

One of the things these numbers tell us is that the best salespeople are spending a combined 65 percent of their sales time finding ideas to talk about and people to talk about those ideas with—and then talking with them. That is what the prospecting and presentation phase is, especially in the key accounts environment. You are basically finding a few things to talk about with a whole bunch of people, and following through on the discussions that move forward.

TIMES SQUARE

19

Suppose you were standing in the middle of Times Square at noon. And suppose you put your hand out and just stood there expectantly. Do you think that, after awhile, somebody would come along and put some money in your hand?

Well, of course, with all the people who walk through Times Square in New York City, it's a pretty good bet that if you simply stood there for long enough, *eventually* somebody would, in fact, put money in your hand. Now here is another question. Would you make *more* money if you held out a cup instead?

If you enhanced the process, would you make more money than if you didn't enhance the process? And, of course, the answer is yes. Why? Well, the cup symbolizes what you are after, what you are trying to get accomplished. By putting the cup out there, it is clear that you are asking for money.

Now suppose you added a sign with the cup, a sign that said "Help." Would this sign, coupled with the cup, accrue more money than just the cup all by itself? Of course it would. Every time you enhance the process you make more money.

Now suppose you had a cup, a sign, and a bell. Even more money? Sure. How about a cup, a sign, a bell, and you start making eye contact with people and walking after them and saying, "Please help me?" With those five things together you are definitely going to make more money than you would if you simply stood there holding out your hand.

I use that example when I am training salespeople who do not necessarily have a lot of experience in dealing with key accounts. I tell it to make a point, as follows:

There is a man in Times Square right now who sells a fake leather business card case. He holds it in front of himself, and as people walk by he simply says, "Want to buy, want to buy, want to buy, want to buy, want to buy."

At the end of the day a chauffeur-driven limousine picks him up and takes him home. Now, what has he figured out? Well, he figured out that if he stands in Times Square this tactic is going to work. Why? Times Square has 42 million people a year walking through it. He knows that if he just stands there long enough, paying no attention at all to the last three Ps in that sequence we just learned—the presentation, product knowledge, and personal development—if he just simply prospected and said, "Want to buy, want to buy, want to buy, want to buy, want to buy," among the 42 million people walking past, enough people would buy.

The people that I'm training ask, "So? What's the point?"

The point is this. If they could talk to 42 million people, that alone would give them what they needed, and they also would not have to be concerned with the last three Ps on the list.

Although people talk about sales being a numbers game, it isn't really, because salespeople cannot actually reach 42 million people. Certainly in the key accounts environment, too, the number of people that you can reach out to is not unlimited. The point is that we have to balance our prospecting with everything else. We cannot simply assume that what we sell has an infinite number of new people to whom we can sell. We have to focus on other things, too.

By the way, just as an aside, think about how that Times Square story relates to the numbers that I told you about my average daily selling routine. Putting my hand out is analogous to the dials. That is one of the things that I need to do to make more sales. But, remember, we said dials are just one of five ratios that I can improve.

- Dials

- Dials to completed calls

- Completed calls to new appointments

- Visits to sales

- Bigger sales

Hand, cup, bell, sign, walking after people—these are five different elements of the story and they correspond to the five different things that you can do to increase your sales. Notice that the majority of these five things (the first three) hinge on my ability to move on and find something new.

That's the case in the key account setting—the setting where we are expected to develop additional business. People don't really prospect enough. They may do plenty of presentations, but they just do not do enough of the prospecting as we have defined it here.

To illustrate why people do not prospect, I have to share some more numbers with you, so bear with me as I break this down in terms of numbers below.

20 : 5 : 1

In general, for every twenty people we prospect to or twenty new ideas we discuss, of those, five will become real prospects and one of those five prospects will turn into a sale.

If you look at 20:5:1, how many yes answers do you see? There is only one yes, really. In essence, that is what everything is pointing toward. How many no answers do you see? Well, of course the answer is nineteen. Whether those answers are from an account that I have worked with before or a brand-new account, those no answers do not necessarily use the word *no*. They may sound like this:

"Sounds great. Call me back next week."

Some of the no's sound like this:

Click.

There are all kinds of ways that people say no to us. Ultimately though, there is going to be something around the order of nineteen no's to get to one yes.

Now, why do I tell you this? Because some salespeople think they can skip all the no's *and go right to the one yes.* That system that gave us nineteen no's is the exact same system that gave us the one yes. The thing that gave us the nineteen no's was the act of prospecting, the act of moving on, the act of finding something else to match up with. There really is no way to get the yes without the nineteen no's. You cannot skip the no's, although people try to.

How many no's does it take for you to get to a yes? How many no answers have you gotten this week?

I want you start thinking about whether you have accumulated enough no answers. If you did not get enough no answers, you are not going to get enough yes answers. That's just basic math. The more proactive you are, the more effective you are at generating sales, the more no answers you are going to generate.

The first reason that people do not prospect is a fear of the word *no*, which they sometimes call rejection. I hope you understand the process here and understand that, far from us looking at this as rejection, we really have to look at the no as part of the means by which we get to an eventual yes, both within the key account or in any other sales setting.

There is another reason people do not prospect enough and it is related to the concept of time. Here is a timeline.

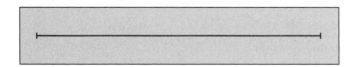

Let's say that the left side is today's date. Pretend it is January 1. Now, I have an eight-week sales cycle. So what is the date eight weeks from that? It is going to be something like February 28 or March 1.

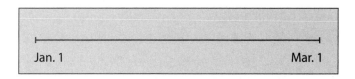

Suppose my entire week was so busy doing things other than finding new ways to implement something inside my key accounts that I never got to any new business development with any of those accounts. Could I still get a sale this week? Even though I did not do any work to try to develop a proposal for any one of my key accounts?

The answer is yes. Of course, I could get a sale this week based on work that I did some time earlier. In fact, when would I really have begun work on that sale? If I closed a sale on January 1, when would I really have begun the process? In my case that would have been eight weeks earlier because I have an eight-week selling cycle. That means that in my sale, it would have been in October that I began that attempt to sell some type of new program within my base of key accounts.

On October 1, I picked up the phone and called Jim Jamison at Hugeco International, and I told him, "You know what, Jim? I was just thinking about you and your company. I'd like to get together with you and figure out what's on your agenda this year, and what you're trying to do with your team." I did that in October and I closed a deal with the company on the 1st of January. But, it looks like I did not prospect, and then as a result of that, I got a sale from one of my key accounts!

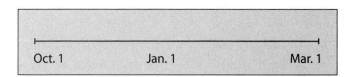

If I'm not careful, I could fool myself into thinking that the very act of not picking up the phone on January 1 was what led to me closing that deal! Actually, I planted the seed in October, which resulted in the sale in January.

Not the case.

Here is the real question: If I do not prospect today, what do I absolutely, positively know will happen to my sales at the end of my sales cycle? Nothing! Do I have to wait until that very day to figure that out, or should I know that now? Well, I should know it now!

Anything that happens in terms of your closing a sale happens as a result of a series of discussions. Those series of discussions have a statistically definable calendar link. If you are operating without knowing what that link is, without knowing what the ratios are, you really are working in the dark. You really do not know how many new points of initiating a discussion it takes for you to develop a single prospect, and you do not know how many of those prospects within your key account base actually turn into business. I encourage you right now to take a look at your own sales pattern and figure out how many initial meetings you scheduled. How many of those meetings actually turned into live discussions? How many of those live discussions actually turned into customers? What was the average timeframe? Once you figure out those numbers, you will be in a better position to implement what you learn in this book.

Focus every day on the end of your sell cycle, because today is the last day to affect the end of your sell cycle.

You may *never* feel like prospecting to track down entirely new deals within your key account base. However, you will always want to get paid!

UPS AND DOWNS

Here's another reason people do not prospect enough within their key accounts: the ups and downs of selling.

If you had 100 prospects, would you expect to close all of them? The answer is obviously no, but let us say you closed twenty of those 100.

If you did that, you would be closing 1 out of 5, which is not a bad ratio. There is nothing inherently good or bad about it, but watch this. If you closed one out of five, in order to close the twenty prospects out of the total of 100 in your base, how many prospects would you have to go through? Obviously, the answer is 100. Let's look at another way of analyzing that.

When I ask salespeople how many prospects they have, most of them will tell me twenty. So let's say a salesperson is selling on the order of 1 out of 5. Suppose I work that group of prospects, and make a sale. Then what would happen?

I would actually lose five prospects! Not right away, not perhaps in an obvious way, but based on the ratio, I really do have only fifteen active prospects left. All my other income has to come from those fifteen active prospects. Yet it doesn't feel like that's how many I have. It feels like I have nineteen active prospects. *That's an illusion!* From the point of view of the closing ratios, which is what we care about, there are really only fifteen left.

So instead of being down to nineteen, which I might think from my base of twenty prospects, I am down to fifteen. It just may not look like that yet, and it certainly does not feel like that. What it feels like is nineteen. Not only that, it feels like a pretty good nineteen because I just closed a sale out of it. What I am likely to emotionally believe about that situation will not typically trigger my urgency to prospect more. So if I believe I have nineteen prospects, I will be less likely to reach out to new people in my base of key accounts to discuss new business.

That means prospecting is going to be a lower priority for me than if I knew that I had zero prospects that were active! If I honestly think I have got nineteen prospects, I do not have any particular urgency to pick up the phone and call anybody.

Alas, I really only have fifteen. In working that group, I will, in fact, produce another sale from that fifteen, and when I do, I will get down to ten. It may not look like ten yet because the prospects do not instantly vanish at the moment I close the sale but, the number of prospects that I count on from that base is really down to ten.

What does it look like I have? It looks like I have eighteen. It feels like eighteen prospects are still on the stove for me. Then I make another sale. I go down to five. It feels like 17. Again, I have no particular need to pick up the phone and call anybody. I am not feeling any urgency.

Now if I make another sale, I am down to zero, and it is usually at that point that the prospects will, in fact, start hurtling down the drain in a way I can actually notice. The law of averages will catch up with me, and I will start to realize that I actually have nothing in the pipeline. That is when I will start to panic, and I will go crazy trying to build my prospect base back up. This is when I will start making the calls. I will get back up to twenty, and I will repeat the whole process again. Over time, the pattern of sales closed resembles a wavy curve continuously going up and down.

As you can imagine, that kind of income pattern is a very stressful cycle. That's the ups and downs of selling. Why does it happen? Because we run out of a sufficient number of prospects that produce sales. In this scenario, what we needed to do upon making the first sale is replace the first sale with five prospects, not one prospect but *five* prospects! Had I done that, I could have maintained my base of twenty all the way across the line. Let me just call a timeout here. I am not suggesting that twenty is the magic number. I am simply using that number for illustration purposes. But whatever number of active prospects I need to maintain, I need to maintain it *at all times.*

Admittedly, that's extremely difficult to do in the real world. Wouldn't it be great if I could develop some kind of an early warning system—a system that alerted me whenever I was in danger of starting the ups-and-downs cycle again?

PART

THE SYSTEM

THE TRIANGLE

21

Here's another way to look at that prospects-leading-up-to-closed-business idea:

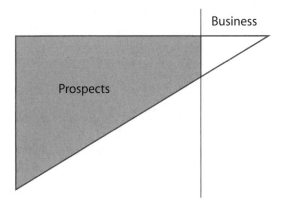

It's a big triangle. Those people to the left are all the *prospective* pieces of business within your key accounts—the people who are giving you Next Steps and working within your average selling cycle—who have a statistically likely shot at eventually turning into customers. Look at it, and you'll realize that the shaded part is what makes the customers *possible*.

Next, we are going to categorize those prospects in three categories: ones, twos, and threes. People in this base do go through stages, after all, and we want to be able to understand the different levels of commitment as a piece of business progresses in its likelihood of closing.

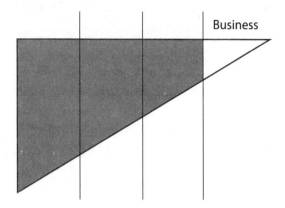

Off to the left of our prospect base, we have our appointments. These are the meetings we schedule to get on the prospect's radar screen to discuss new business. Notice that we can call this column the "First Appointment or "initial contact" column if we want. Whatever we call it, we understand that it can be used to measure the times we begin the process of discussing a project, product, or service.

Note: Sometimes the label "First Appointment" is a little distracting to people. They assume that it means you can never have had any contact with the company, or the primary contact beforehand for the meeting to count as a "First Appointment." We schedule First Appointments with our current customers all the time. As long as it goes on the person's calendar as an upcoming meeting, and as long as the potential for working on something new is on the agenda, it counts. You can call this column whatever you want, however.

To the left of that are our opportunities. These are people with whom we don't yet have a First Appointment (FA) to talk about new business, and who have not given us any kind of Next Step. (Most of the people salespeople instinctively consider prospects are in fact *opportunities*.)

If I am conducting a training program with people who are getting ready to use this system for the first time, I will turn to one of the people in the room at this point, and I will say "Okay, Mr. First Participant, tell me about a company you're working with. The ABC Company, good. All right, I need to know where in this picture the ABC Company should fall. Is it here in the shaded part of the triangle, is it a closed sale (Business), is it First Appointment, or is it an opportunity?"

In other words, I want to know if that company can be categorized as what we call a prospect, which is not necessarily what the participant would call a prospect.

I really do need to know that, so now I will ask the group as a whole some pointed questions. I will say "Okay, he told us the ABC Company was his best prospect, what do you think is the first question I would ask about ABC?"

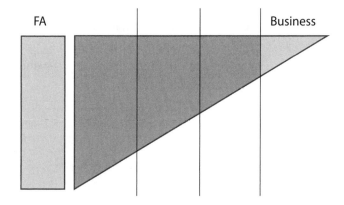

There are a lot of possible answers, but there's really only one right answer. I let them ask and ask and ask until they come across something relevant, and then at a certain point, I will reengage in the conversation. I will say, "Let me ask you this: when did you start talking to this person about this particular opportunity?"

Look at it again. We said a prospect is a prospect by virtue of the conversation playing out within our normal selling cycle. Therefore, "When was the first discussion with this prospect about this particular opportunity?" becomes a very important question.

If I ask, "When was the first meeting to discuss this particular piece of business?" and I have not even had a meeting yet to discuss any add on business at all, well, obviously it cannot be in the active prospect category! It goes into the opportunity (O) column.

What is my next question to the group about the ABC Company? Let us assume that we know that the first meeting was a month ago. Well, another critical question is going to be, "When did I last speak with or meet with this person?"

That will tell me whether things actually have been moving forward and how long it has been since I had some kind of forward motion in the sale. If the first time I ever spoke with this person was a month ago, and the most recent time I spoke to this person was also a month ago, then I guess that means there has not been any progress since then. There is no forward progress happening. Clearly, it does not match our criteria of a prospect because there has not been forward movement in the process. The person is not playing ball with us. Back it goes into the opportunity column.

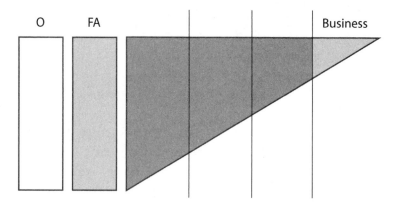

Here's the third (and, I hope, obvious) question I am going to ask: "When are you scheduled to speak with this person next?" The answer to that is going to tell me whether this person really belongs on the board at all. If I do not have some kind of Next Step scheduled, if I do not have some kind of forward meeting happening, some kind of spot on the other person's calendar, then this lead really does not match my criteria for what constitutes a prospect.

If you don't have a scheduled time to discuss something that you both agree will help to move the sales cycle forward, then you've got nothing.

(Note: Sometimes people ask me, "Does it count if I've scheduled a phone meeting to touch base with this person?" Here's the answer. If you routinely, or even occasionally, close sales over the phone, then yes, it does count as a prospect. If your business must almost always be closed in person, then no, you should not count that person as a prospect.)

Here's another, parallel, question I'll ask the group in order to clarify where a prospect belongs. "What is the Next Step they have agreed to?" In other words, what ball have you tossed out? What did you get them to agree to that would advance the sale?"

Take a look once again at those questions:

> *When was the first meeting to talk about this piece of business?* ("Well, I never actually met with them to talk about this piece of business." Guess what? ***This is not a prospect!***)

> *When did you last speak to them?* ("Well, it was about six months ago, and my selling cycle is four weeks." Similarly—***this is not a prospect!***)

> *When are you going back?* What's the Next Step the other person has agreed to? ("Well, I'm waiting to hear about when a good time for us to get together is." Similarly, ***this is not a prospect!***)

We have to pose these questions, and appeal to these standards, in order to impose our definition of the word *prospect* on our base of business. Admittedly, this is a very rigid and very strict definition of prospect, but it is better to determine without any ambiguity whether or not there is some kind of commitment to moving the sale forward. That's better than erring on the side of assuming that there will be a commitment probably, maybe, or someday, we hope.

We have found that when people assume there is going to be a commitment, probably, maybe, someday, they hope, then they are all too frequently disappointed.

Let me add to your list one more specific question to ask in order to determine whether or not we're actually looking at a prospect. It sounds like this:

In your view, what is the very next thing that must happen in order to eventually close the sale—and when will that happen?

During our training programs, I really do ask people to write that down word for word and take a good, long, hard look at it. It is the kind of question that is easy to lose sight of in the hustle and bustle of keeping track of a bunch of different contacts and a bunch of different accounts. You can get so tied up in the technicalities and so tied up in the new introductions and in the specifics of the product offerings, that you lose sight of the fact that there really is something specific that needs to happen for any given sale to move toward closure. You could do worse than making a daily habit of asking that question about any prospect that makes it into the active prospect portions of your system.

A BETTER WAY TO MOVE THE SALES CYCLE FORWARD

Here once again is that all-important question I am urging you to analyze for any and every active prospect in your base of key accounts:

What is the very next thing that must happen for you to eventually close the sale—and when will that happen?

Let's say that the very next thing that has to happen for me to close a sale within a given key account is to get together with the prospect (you) and go over an outline, or preliminary proposal of how we might be able to work together. (This is basically a preview of my full-scale proposal, a concise version of the major assumptions I'm working under. My goal is to get you to scribble all over it and give me (a) correct information and (b) some "insider" language I can use in the final document.)

Well, at the end of the meeting, I say that. I say, "You've given me a lot to think about. Let's get together again so I can show you an outline or overview of how we might be able to work together on this project. Can we meet next Tuesday at 2:00 P.M.?" When I say that, something interesting is going to happen because you the prospect have to respond, either positively or negatively.

If I toss out the ball to you and ask you to agree to that, you will either agree or not agree to that Next Step. If you do not agree to meet with me to take a look at that outline, or you do not agree to do so in a certain time frame that works for me, then I am not as likely to get that sale than if you had said yes, you would meet with me next Tuesday at 2:00 P.M. That is just a fact of sales math.

This system is all about tracking the likelihood of closing in your key accounts. We're going to be focusing in on this kind of sales math.

During the training program, I would ask the person, "When are you going to go back?" The person might say, "I'm going back next Tuesday at 2:00 P.M." As the trainer, I'm not going to stop there, I am going to continue by saying, "Great. What do *they* think you are going to do at that meeting?"

Does what *they* think is going happen at that meeting match up with the very next thing *you* think has to happen for you to close the sale? If those two sets of expectations are totally different, then you still have some work to do. While you're doing that work, you will want to think about removing that person from the active prospect section of the board, or at least strategizing on a better way to move this opportunity forward.

That's usually what we're looking at: a reason to strategize a better way to move the sales cycle forward. Very often, when people come to us and say they have problems with their closing ratios, what they really mean is that they have the intention to close business, but they are simply not very good at communicating why they think the business is worth closing. This causes the prospect to have a very different view on what is going to happen next. The salesperson tries to implement these closing techniques that are supposed to trick the prospect into agreeing to close when he does not know that is what is going to happen. Of course, that does not happen very often, and the only way you are going to pull off that sale is if you would normally get the sale anyway. (Remember the "Rule of One-Third"!)

By asking these kinds of questions in a focused way, we begin to realize that the simple fact that someone worked with us in the past *does not* mean that he is a prospect right now. People who have not really taken the steps necessary for them to qualify as a prospect simply don't belong in the shaded active prospect area, as in the diagram on page 72. We shouldn't think of them as prospects, and we shouldn't invest time in them as if they were prospects. Perhaps most important of all, we shouldn't forecast income from them as if they were prospects.

As a team, we should all share common words that we use a lot to describe a prospect. *Not* sharing a common definition of a prospect, and a common philosophy for allocating time to prospects, is a huge problem.

Why do I say that? Because, paradoxically enough, the narrower your definition of a prospect, the more money you are going to make.

Think about it. If hardly anything gets into that triangle that we use to prioritize our day, if the only thing that lands there is solid discussions that really are likely, statistically, to turn into sales, that means everything else is not getting in there for us to waste our time on. Our goal is to maintain a base of prospects that really do represent high percentage shots for future business. By excluding all the other junk from that triangle and not spending a lot of time and energy and effort on those people who are not yet helping us to move through the sales process, we are going to maximize our effort and turn more of those discussions into commission checks.

The only legitimate way we can expand that triangle is by getting really solid prospects to put into it. Usually that means calling our key accounts and asking for referrals or asking to meet with them personally. (I'll show you some strategies for doing that in Chapter 65.)

What happens if we guess wrong or we categorize our prospects against these questions, and they really are interested in new business? That means that we are going to have more sales than we would otherwise had forecasted! That is better than having fewer sales than you imagine or forecast you are going to have.

KEY ACCOUNT CATEGORIES—
HUNDREDS AND ZEROES

Now it's time to think about how to get clear criteria for what's in our triangle, and how to understand the standards for what is going to go in these three categories.

Let me show you how this works by, in a sense, combining everything we have talked about so far. What do we know about the sales process? We know that there are four steps to it, and that the last step, the close, is the one we're ultimately moving toward.

What do these mean? We have to *open* or qualify. We have to do an *interviewing* phase. We have to make a *presentation*, and we have to *close* the sale. We can therefore relabel the boxes this way: O, I, P, C.

We also know that the closer we get to the close the closer we get to 100 percent. So I want to put 100 percent over in the far right-hand corner.

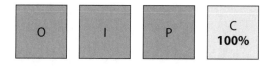

Any piece of business that we do—bill or receive money—whether it is from a brand-new customer or (more likely in our case, since we're talking about key accounts) somebody we worked with previously—we are going to call 100 percent. That's one end of the spectrum. At the other end of the spectrum will be, obviously, zero percent. That's even *before* I start the first phase of the process, of course, so that's where I'm going to mark it.

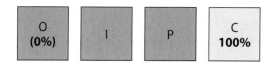

Who would these zero percent people be? These would be the opportunities we talked about a little bit earlier. They could be former prospects. They could be people who have fallen back, who used to be in that group of active prospects, but then became inactive. Or they could be candidates, suspects, leads, targets, whatever you want to call people within the key account whom you have not yet spoken with about a particular piece of business.

24

KEY ACCOUNT CATEGORIES— BETWEEN ZERO AND ONE HUNDRED

Somewhere between our zero percent people and our 100 percent are our prospects for new business in our key accounts in the middle.

The best way to understand why is to go to the 50 percent point. I have gone to find the far right-hand end, and I have gone to find the far left-hand end, and have covered those two extremes. Now, I can tell you from personal experience, having trained salespeople on this material thousands upon thousands of times, that the very easiest point of entry into the system is to look next at the stuff that is exactly in the middle. Let's do that.

Prospect Management as it applies to the key account is actually quite simple. Our active prospects lie in one of three "pots": *50 percent, better than 50 percent, and less than 50 percent.* The active prospects for new business fall out of the system over time, but some of them, of course, actually do reach 100 percent and produce new revenue for us.

Basically, if I understand 50 percent I understand everything else. Yet the fifty percent is initially hard for some people to understand.

Most salespeople seem to believe that if there is any chance at all of something happening, it has a 50 percent chance. That's an illusion. Let me give you an example of the way that people use this illusory standard to identify when something has a 50 percent chance of closing.

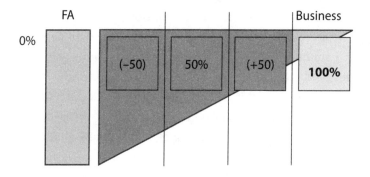

If I show a proposal to somebody, it is possible they will say yes to what I propose, and it is possible they will say no. So it may be tempting to think that the odds for closing the deal would be 50/50. But if you think about it, that really is not an accurate label. After all, if you buy a lottery ticket, it is possible it is a winner and it is possible that you're going to lose the dollar you spent on it. So there are two options here, too, but I do not think you would want to go around making spending decisions on the assumption that there is a 50/50 chance you are going to win six million dollars tomorrow night.

In fact, the odds are *not* 50/50 for winning the lottery ticket. They are more on the order of a million to one. By the same token, the simple fact that there are two possible outcomes when we are showing someone a proposal doesn't mean we've got a 50/50 chance of closing new business with that account. The odds might not be a million to one, but they aren't 50/50 percent, either, just because there's a possible yes and a possible no.

When something falls into the 50 percent category, it has to mean *more* than simply two possible outcomes. There has to be as equal a chance of a yes answer as of a no answer. In a direct sale, which is to say a sale where the salesperson is meeting directly with the decision maker, and excluding situations where you are dealing with brokers and third-parties, there are really four conditions that make the sale fall into the 50 percent category in the Prospect Management System.

The first of the four criteria for inclusion of the 50 percent column is that we are speaking and finally presenting to the right person or right people. I am quite happy using the term *decision maker*, but I want you to understand too that when I use this term I am including within that category the people who could get the decision made. I am taking a very pragmatic approach on that score. Whatever you call this person, it has to be the right person or the right group of people to talk to: the individual or group who can either make the decision or get the decision made.

Here is the second criterion: I have to be at the stage of the sale where I really have learned what the potential clients do, why they do it, who they're currently doing it with, and so on—and I have to be showing them a plan that I honestly believe could help them do it better. In other words, I am showing them the right plan. Now, by right plan I mean a plan that is based on what they are actually trying to get accomplished, something that really can help them do what they are trying to do better than how they are doing it right now. I'm looking at something that I think should really make sense for this situation.

The third criterion is that I know I am working with the right budget. If I go to a person who has spending authority of $5,000, and I show them a plan that they love, and that would be perfect for them, but that costs $10,000—guess what? That is more than they have the authority to spend. It's not the right budget, yet. How do I get the sale? I will either have to change the plan, change the budget, or incorporate somebody else into the decision.

That's three of the four criteria for a 50-percent prospect. Before we get to the fourth, however, I have to give you a little more information about the word *right*.

SOME BACKGROUND ON
THE WORD *RIGHT*

Let me give you a little bit of background on these first three criteria. When I say the word *right*—as in right person, right plan, and right budget, I don't mean right in some abstract sense, or right as in morally right. I mean right as in *righted*, as in the other person having actually *corrected* me about something important.

This principle of being righted is something that is closely connected to the idea of throwing out the ball. In other words, I am going to keep tossing out ways, suggestions, ideas, principles, and initiatives, and I am going to want to see how much correcting I can get the other person to do to what I am proposing.

If it's not dynamic, if there's not some kind of give-and-take happening, I haven't been righted. I do not want the person to just sit there like a lump throughout the information-gathering phase and give me no reaction. Instead, I am going to constantly challenge my own assumptions and see if the other person will join in challenging those assumptions with me.

(By the way, in this book, we will spend a lot more time on developing those questions that will help you "get righted" and gather the appropriate information.)

This idea of being righted during the sales process is a lot easier to pull off than it may sound. There is a natural human tendency to correct other people. Sometimes, during a training program, I will point to someone who's relatively new to the group and say, "You know, when we opened up this program you told me that you had been in sales for nine years." Well, instantly the person will correct me and say, "No, no, I did not say I had been with the organization for nine years. What I said was that I had gotten hired by the organization six months ago."

This is a perfect example of the getting-righted principle. When I want to find out some way to determine what the situation is, I will often give the prospect the opportunity to correct me in much the same way, by throwing out a piece of information that I am not quite 100 percent sure about, then asking if I have it right. The person's natural inclination to correct me will take over.

That is a lot of what we are talking about in the information gathering phase and definitely something we want to make sure has happened by the time the prospect gets to that middle, or 50-percent, column.

Here's why it's so important. People prefer correcting you over creating something brand-new. They would much rather tell the salesperson where he went wrong than help develop an outline or a series of bullet points that the proposal should actually be focused on.

That's fine. We have no problem with that. We are going to make our own assumptions, and we are going to let the person correct us and point us in exactly the right direction. The fact is, as soon as I know I am wrong, I am right, or at least righted. In fact, I am not really right—I am righted! I do not even really know that I am right until I have given you a chance to correct me and you have either signed off on what I did or told me where I needed to do some more work.

THE FOURTH CRITERION

26

I told you there were four criteria for entry into the 50-percent column. We've already discussed the first three. The final criterion is having the right timetable for implementation.

By that I mean our timetable. From the moment I present to the right person about the right budget with the right plan, how long will it take from that point to a verbal decision? In other words, how does the timing for closing this deal compare to the timing for closing my average deal?

Sometimes when I mention the right timetable people assume that I am talking about the timetable for implementing the product or service. I actually prefer to look at it in terms of timetables that I as a salesperson am following. (Of course, it is okay for you to make sure you are talking about a timetable that works for the other person, but this is not as relevant to your selling cycle as knowing whether or not the discussion you are having fits into the average selling cycle for your company.)

I really have to be sure that my sale is unfolding within my own ideal timeframe, my typical selling cycle, or at least, I have to make sure that this prospect does not violate that sales cycle in any dramatic way.

Sometimes when I bring this up as a criterion for inclusion within the 50 percent category, people suddenly become very defensive about the whole notion of an average selling cycle. Maybe they weren't very defensive about it when it came up in the abstract, but they are defensive when I try to get them to adopt this as a standard. When I run into people who have this kind of reaction to what I am proposing here, I ask this question:

If you look back on just those cases where you eventually closed the sale, how long did it take you to go from a presentation to a verbal decision?

Notice that I am not asking now about the entire sales process, just about the amount of time that it is likely to take this person to get from the point where we are at our presentation to the final decision. If it looks like it is going to be another nine months, and it typically only takes us two weeks to get from this point to the decision, then we will know we have a problem and we cannot put it in the 50-percent category.

The fact is I very seldom see anything take longer than three or four weeks to go from a presentation to a final decision, and one or two weeks is even more likely. (The only exception involves people who sell things to municipal, state, or local governments.)

TO THE RIGHT OF CENTER

27

Let's look in more depth at this "Better Than" category. It's the one right before the closed business.

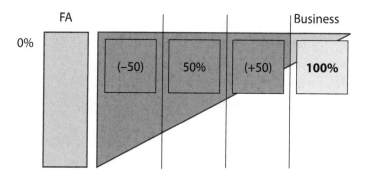

Suppose you make a presentation, and the next day, the customer calls up and says, "You really got what we were talking about. We were passing your presentation around to everyone. We all love it. We think it's in great shape. It's exactly what we want to do. The price looks fine. We're going to go ahead. Let's start next week."

That's a verbal yes.

Here's a question. Once the prospect has given you that verbal agreement, would you call that a 100 percent sale?

Well, not quite. We haven't got a contract yet.

Would you say it's better than 50 percent?

Sure. It is definitely better than 50, it's just not quite 100.

In this system, we arbitrarily call that kind of prospect 90 percent, based on the theory that 9 out of 10 times that somebody makes a verbal commitment to you something will happen. Even though 90 percent is better than 50 percent, it's not quite a closed sale.

Now, there is also a timeframe for that portion of the sale. How long does it take to go from the verbal yes to actually closing the sale? Note that I am not asking how long it should take for that to happen, and I am not asking how long it took one remarkable time that everyone remembers because that period of time was so unusual. I'm asking what happens most of the time.

In the majority of cases, how long does it take to go from 90 percent to closed, to the point where I have a purchase order, a letter of agreement, or a contract. Whatever that average amount of time is, you should be able to identify it in your key accounts environment.

Suppose the prospect said, "This sounds great. I'm ready to go."

Suppose the salesperson then said, "That's wonderful. When do you think we can wrap up the contracts?"

Then suppose the prospect said in response, "Well, I'm thinking it will be probably be about five months." And normally it takes three days.

Is that 90 percent? By my way of thinking it would not be. Why not? Because we want to look at what the normal pattern is. We would be a lot more comfortable if the person said, "It's going to be between two and four days." If they say *five months*, instantly we as salespeople feel a strange kind of disconnect, like something's not right. When you feel a little bit of discomfort like that, it's a tip-off. It's something you listen to. It means this isn't really an active prospect.

TO THE LEFT OF CENTER

28

At the end of my first meeting with a prospective buyer, my pattern is to say something like the following, "Why don't we get together again next Tuesday at 2:00 P.M. so I can show you an outline of how we might be able to work together?"

Now, suppose I came back, as scheduled, but as I left that second meeting, I still needed to learn one or more of the things that qualify as the criteria of the 50-percent category. In other words, I still was not quite sure if I was dealing with the right person. I still was not sure I had the right plan. I still was not sure if I had the right budget and I still was totally in the dark about what the time limits were for the decision. Would you call that kind of a meeting better than zero percent?

Sure! Because I have a scheduled Next Step, don't I?

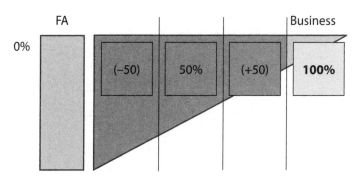

But would you call it 50 percent? Well, by definition we can't call it 50 percent, because it is missing one or more of those criteria. But we could call it less than 50 percent, or almost 50 percent, or not quite 50 percent.

We arbitrarily call the prospects in this category 25 percent. And when we say that, all we mean is: We have had a First Appointment or first discussion and we now have a next scheduled step to meet in order to gain more information.

TO THE LEFT OF THAT . . .

What did I have just before getting to that 25 percent phase? Well, just before that I set up the first meeting. Now I have what we call a First Appointment.

When I say First Appointment or FA, what I mean is the meeting is set but I have not yet met with the person. I have scheduled a first meeting to discuss either a new piece of business with an existing customer or a brand new meeting with somebody at a whole new organization. In either case, the meeting is set. We just have not had it yet.

So if I make a meeting for next Tuesday at 2:00 P.M., and the person agrees at that moment, the sale goes into the FA column at the far left.

But suppose I went to that meeting and the person was not there. It was a no show. My sale now is *not* getting closer to, it is getting further away from, closing. Let's go look at another scenario.

Let's say I am going back to get the decision from someone. Well, I still put that at 50 percent because I have gathered all the information I can and there is a clear indication I have all four of those criteria, at least I think I do. Accordingly, I am going to assume it is a 50 percent chance of me getting either a yes or no.

Suppose I am going back to pick up the contract after the person gave me a verbal commitment? I am going to call that a 90 percent prospect.

If I have already closed the sale, then obviously it goes to 100 percent.

30 THE FAR EDGE

To the left of the FA column, of course, is the opportunity column, the group that can't qualify for placement anywhere else on the board.

In terms of managing your key accounts, everything is either an opportunity (O) (which includes fallbacks from the other categories), an FA (a First Appointment or first meeting to discuss the new piece of business), a 25 percent (which means I met with the person once and I have a scheduled Next Step to gather more information), a 50 percent (I have all four of the critical criteria in place), a 90 percent (I have all that stuff from 50 percent and a verbal commitment) . . . or a closed (I just picked up the contract or got the signed purchase order). That is 100 percent.

That's the whole system. Nothing you do to generate revenue should be unclassifiable. Everything will fit into one, and only one, of those categories.

THE DISCONNECT

31

So picture this. I'm leading this training program. Everybody in the room is nodding their heads. They're going "Got it. Couldn't be simpler." At that stage they understand I have simply restated what I laid out in the beginning, which is that people fall out of your prospect base through time. I have added a bit more detail into the categories that match up with each of these three active prospect categories. Everybody appears very comfortable with these criteria. But then there's a disconnect. After I go over the criteria, I break the participants into small groups. I give them a series of scenarios and ask them to rank each of them according to the system that we just learned. The groups all give different answers.

What does that tell me?

Well, it says two things. The first is that people maybe are not listening as closely in the training program as perhaps they might. The second but just as important is that people really do hold on tightly to their current definition of what a prospect is. The definition is unique to them. A prospect may be defined as "somebody I really want to do business with," even though that person may not have agreed to any kind of Next Step.

Don't fall victim to the disconnect. Learn the criteria, use them, and challenge someone else to see how well you've actually applied them to your base business. My experience is that people really do need a colleague to challenge them on these standards in order to apply them consistently to their own key accounts contacts.

The moral: Don't try to go it alone! Get a sales manager or a colleague to look over your classifications. Do the same for him or her. Challenge one another's assumptions about what should go where and why. The system really does work better that way.

ADAPTING THE SYSTEM TO MULTIPLE PRODUCTS AND SERVICES

I place a great deal of emphasis in determining the overall sales cycle, and also in determining the average amount of time it takes somebody to move from FA to 25, from 25 to 50, from 50 to 90, and from 90 to closed. Violation of the average sales cycle is a good reason not to consider that lead an active prospect. That means that the salesperson can't project income from that lead. (Having an active prospect fall back to the Opportunity column sometimes galvanizes a salesperson, offering plenty of motivation to prove that the sales manager is wrong to put the deal in fallback. That's a victory, too, because creating that kind of "I'll show you" motivation is a completely positive outcome.)

Sometimes I will train salespeople to use this system to sell many different things. In those situations, I try and focus in on the average sale for a particular product and we use one or two of those for examples. We will not try and nail down all the possible situations for a different product with a different sales cycle. We're looking for the average sales cycle, for what usually happens when they're trying to sell this particular product or service. Even though we may be dealing with different time frames and there are different products and product mixes, we always want to identify the average selling cycle for the particular situation that we are in.

If I don't know the averages, I have to assume personal responsibility for finding out.

After a while, very scientifically, by monitoring all of the prospects on the board, I am going to get a personal sense of what my actual selling cycle is in any given situation. Then, I am going to compare each and every new sale to that, and strategize accordingly. I want to be able to compare each sale that I am working on to a relevant historical average; then, based upon that, I want to constantly be asking myself, does it fit the pattern or not. If it doesn't, what can I do to help move it forward, what worked in a similar situation?

Think about it. If we look at the total number of potential sales that we work on over the course of a year, we realize that the majority of them do not close. That means only a minority will match this pattern of forward movement. Now, the advantage of conducting this form of analysis is that we identify the pattern that takes place in the ones that we do derive most of the income from.

That is why it is worthwhile to hold our activity, to apply these relatively strict and admittedly rigorous criteria to determining whether something is moving along quickly enough before we invest our time and effort and energy in it. We want to recognize the difference between the pattern that usually leads to revenue for us and for the company and the pattern that usually does not.

The pattern that usually does not lead to income is typically the one that drags on forever, the one where we do not have any real commitment from the other side. We want to do everything we possibly can to avoid that lead. We don't want to find ourselves continuously saying, "This one is different for such-and-such a reason, and this one is different for this other reason."

CRITERIA AND QUESTIONS FOR EACH KEY ACCOUNT CATEGORY

Use these criteria and questions to work backward from closed and challenge your own assessment of what's really happening in your own key account base.

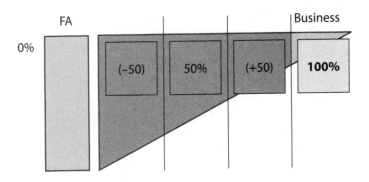

90 Percent

Ranking Criteria

❏ Verbal agreement
❏ Contract on desk

Strategy Question

❑ When will this plan close? (Need definite date.)

Overall Key Account Management Questions

❑ Can you schedule any FAs near these closing appointments?
❑ Does the prospect know they're closing?
❑ Is this meeting merely to close or is it to advance the sale by beginning implementation?
❑ What specific plan(s) has been selected? Do we have a verbal commitment to do new business within this account?
❑ Compared to the 50-percent column, does this column indicate closing, presentation, or ranking problems?
❑ Is any prospect in this column too old?
❑ Do we have a 90 percent chance of closing these deals?

50 Percent

Ranking Criteria

❑ Presenting to right person with right presentation, right budget, right timetable.

Strategy Questions

❑ What is the deal worth?
❑ Need specific dollar amount.
❑ When will they decide?
❑ How does this compare to our average timeline for decision-making in a deal that reaches this point?
❑ What will it take to move this to 90 percent? When will that happen?
❑ Why are you presenting this proposal? (Why does it make sense for them to do it this way?)
❑ How do we know this person (or people) will be able to make this decision?
❑ When will they decide?

- What is their timetable for implementation?
- Who else are we competing against?
- Has the specific dollar amount been discussed?
- Have the specific plans been discussed?
- Do we have a date to present this, or present this again?
- Do they want this to happen as much as we do?
- What resources/strategies can be utilized to drive these decisions?
- If we're waiting for a decision, can we also prospect for new business within this account?

Overall Key Account Management Questions
- Is the value of these prospects multiplied by 50 percent sufficient to hit short-term income goals?
- What should the average prospect value be?
- If too high, the sales cycle lengthens; if too low, prospecting activity must increase.
- Is any prospect in this column too old?
- Is there a 1 in 2 chance of closing these deals?
- What are the next opportunities within these accounts for more income?
- When should these opportunities be closing?

25 Percent

Ranking Criteria
- Completed FA. Next Step scheduled to gain information.

Strategy Questions
- When was the first meeting?
- When was the last meeting?
- When is the next appointment?
- What will it take to move this prospect to 50 percent?
- How long will that take?

- What would the deal be worth?
- What/how/why/when does this company do what it does?
- Are they buying from/working with anyone else?
- Why that company? How did they choose them?
- Is this company looking at any competitor?
- Why that company?
- Why should this prospect buy from us?
- What are the individual decision makers trying to accomplish?
- Can we help them do it better?

Overall Key Account Management Questions

- What does this column tell us about our recent prospecting activity? A low number would indicate:

    1. Not enough FAs in last two weeks.

    2. Inability to create a Next Step with qualified prospects

    3. Small-size prospects, which skipped the first stage.

    4. Recent FAs were predominantly unqualified (either contact or organization).

- Is any prospect in this column too old?
- Do we have a 1 in 4 chance of closing these deals?

First Appointment (FA)

Ranking Criteria

- Scheduled first meeting to discuss new business with this account (date and time).

Strategy Questions

- Is this the first meeting about this deal?
- Is the meeting set?
- What are most relevant examples of similar success stories we've had at this company?

- ❏ What are most relevant examples of similar success stories we've had elsewhere?
- ❏ Are each day's appointments close together?
- ❏ Are there any leads near any of these appointments, which would make sense to meet on this trip?
- ❏ What Next Step (and fallback) strategy will you use at the end of these meetings?

Overall Key Account Management Question

- ❏ What is the right number of FAs to maintain at all times?

Opportunities/Fallbacks

Ranking Criteria

- ❏ No Next Step
- ❏ No decision expected soon

Strategy Questions

- ❏ Why is there no Next Step?
- ❏ What is happening within the next two weeks?
- ❏ What divisions within any of these opportunities are most like our existing customers? How can we reach out to them
- ❏ Who do our customers buy from and sell to that we can call on?
- ❏ What percentage of our next opportunities are new customers, former customers, and existing customers?

Overall Key Account Management Questions

- ❏ What are the next opportunities to pursue and why?
- ❏ How many, on average, do you need to reach out to in order to generate a single appointment?
- ❏ Are there other contacts within our existing prospects and customers worth pursuing?

34

SOME THOUGHTS ON QUALIFYING

Most people think qualifying is something that happens on the phone, before they allow or accept a First Appointment.

To be sure, this is one way of looking at qualifying. My only problem with that is, if this way is applied thoughtlessly, it has the effect of simply limiting the number of First Appointments you set. Often, that means you have to compensate with a higher number of dials in order to still meet your target number of First Appointments.

The way I look at it, the driving consideration for going or not going on an appointment should be a territory management consideration, and not the fact that you have qualified the lead. In other words, I would rather set up an appointment with somebody who might be able to give me a referral, if that supposedly "unqualified" lead happens to be right next door to somebody I am already meeting in my territory.

I think of qualifying as a decision that the salesperson will make by the end of the first meaningful conversation with someone. This definitely applies to key account strategies because when we are talking about the internal markets within a company—the way that each company breaks down into a number of different companies and opportunities for us to pursue—we want to think about how much effort and energy we want to invest in any given opportunity, as opposed to any other opportunity! We have to be the ones who decide how much time and effort to invest in a given prospect before walking away.

We have to decide early how many meetings or how much time we will devote to getting the sale. In order to do that, we have to answer the following four questions:

1. How big can the sale potentially be and how does that number compare to my average sale?

2. How long will it take for me to close and collect the first dollar on the sale?

3. What kind of resources (time, lost opportunity, or financial expense) will it take for me to close this deal? In other words, how big is my investment going to be here?

4. How realistic is it for me to expect to get this sale through my existing contacts?

You can make a great deal of headway with these questions by using an intelligent qualifying question on the first meeting. Our question sounds like this: "How many salespeople do you have?" If I'm working with a key account of ours, and I come across a smaller subgroup of that account, I am going to find out how many salespeople report to that new contact that I have reached out to. If this person tells me he has ten salespeople, then I know that there will probably be only one or maybe two decision makers working together to make a choice about what kind of training for that group. I already know the usual dollar size of that kind of sale, and I know that it is taking two to three visits over four to eight weeks to close that deal. That is the maximum amount of time the sale should take me.

If, on the other hand, they say they have 150 salespeople, I know that there will be many decision makers, even though eventually the prospect will elect a contact (usually one with my product in their title, like training manager, for example) for me to fully penetrate the account. That is going to be three to five visits over a period of about six to nine weeks and

I will probably need to begin with a pilot program, something that takes two or three visits over a period of two to four weeks to set up.

Now, if they say they have only one or two salespeople, then I am looking at one call to close. If I have to travel to get to them, then it may not be worth it for me to do that. (Then again, it may be worth it, for instance, if I already have a meeting scheduled with someone else who's near that contact.) Again, that is a territory management consideration.

If we decide to move on, then we have to ask ourselves:

- Why can't the sale close today? Even if this is the first meeting of a typically very long sales process, and there is no way it will close in one call, we still need to know why.

- In my view, what is the very next thing needed in order to eventually close the sale?

- When will that happen?

Real qualifying comes from comparing each new sales opportunity to similar opportunities that we have actually closed. We qualify in terms of deciding the potential revenue of sales as well as the number of visits to close and the lessons learned from unclosed sales. Simply meeting a second time or showing a proposal does not necessarily advance the sale. If you stop to think about it, the prospect only advances to 25 percent, *if* after the First Appointment, the prospect has agreed to do the very next thing needed in order to eventually close the sale within my normal sales cycle.

IMPLEMENTATION

35

The beauty of implementing this system, whether you do so on a bulletin board, a spreadsheet, or magnetic board (available through our company), is that once you *do* implement it, as outlined, what you are looking at, if you have followed all of these instructions, is real.

If you've done as I've suggested, you have categorized everything accurately, according to the three active prospect categories—25 percent, 50 percent and 90 percent—and you have found a way to discipline yourself to deal realistically with people who really have not committed to any kind of tangible Next Step with you or who have exceeded your average sales cycle. You put those people back into the opportunity column. By the way, that is not a bad place for them to be. It is a great place because it reminds you that you have to find a way to get them into the active column.

That is a dose of reality, and you now have a better, more accurate snapshot of what actually is happening in your key account base. Now that you know what you have got, you can take the steps necessary to get the board to look right. The game is not really about having a full column in every prospect category. It is more about saying to yourself, "Given my ratios, my average sale size, and my income goals, what should my board look like?" Let me try and create that board and see what it really looks like. Let us put together an action plan so I can take my board from looking the way it looks now to looking right, with the ideal formulations. By the way, the ideal formulation of the board really does look something like this.

One of the best ways to use the Prospect Management System is as a tool for developing sales forecasts. If you are in regular contact with anyone who is a sales manager or if you are a sales manager yourself, you know that the Powers That Be have an annoying way of insisting on projections regarding what kind of income you think is going to be forthcoming for the people that you are selling to for certain specific periods in the future.

It is often very entertaining to simply write down numbers as scenarios that could stand as income projections for these Powers That Be, but doing this tends to erode good will with them and it is not what I would recommend. Instead of doing that, take your updated prospect management board and make a habit of conducting your weekly board review exercise with it, with a commitment to being brutally honest with yourself every step of the way. Once you have done this for two or three weeks, you will be looking at not only a fairly accurate summary of what your current business actually is, but you will also see everything that is in process and is likely to unfold over the coming sales cycle. So let us say the sales cycle is 12 weeks and you have responsibility to deliver a sales projection of the income you are going to produce over that 12-week period. Here is the best way to go about doing it:

1. Assign a dollar value to everything in the 25-percent, 50-percent, and 90-percent columns.

2. Add up all of the dollar values from the prospects that currently show up in your 25-percent column.

3. Repeat the procedure for all of the prospects in your 50-percent column.

4. Add up all of the prospects that show up in your 90-percent column.

5. Multiply the total of the results from the 25-percent column by 25 percent.

6. Multiply the total that showed up from the 50-percent column by 50 percent.

7. Multiply all the results from the 90-percent column by 90 percent. Add this figure together with the modified totals from the 25-percent, 50-percent, and 90-percent columns.

Once you add those final figures together, you will have a more accurate estimate of your income performance over the next 12 weeks than you would have gained by simply identifying your favorite prospects and assuming that they are all going to close. (Which is what most people who deal with key account projections do.) This process delivers a better number to give your sales manager than one based on guesswork, optimism, or a gut feeling. So use it!

PART III

THE MAJOR ACCOUNT

MAJOR ACCOUNTS— AN OVERVIEW

Let's talk specifically about major accounts.

I put this part right after the discussion of prospect management for a reason. Prospect management is typically misunderstood by salespeople who have to deal with major accounts. They think of the system as being something that is connected to a transactional sale, where I try to sell product X to somebody one time and one time only, measuring the progress of where I am with those sales, and I follow it through the various categories.

Sometimes people say to me, "Well, here's the problem. It looks like it would only work if you keep the funnel filled with more and more leads and that you'd need an infinite supply of potential leads, and out of those you'd get some workable number of prospects. And guess what. I've only got two customers."

When somebody tells me they're involved in a major account sale—not just key accounts, regular customers with repeat business, but major accounts—I know that those customers have to be big. They're like American Express or Coca-Cola.

Guess what that means, though? Those huge companies are actually 30 or 40 smaller companies all linked together, sometimes without much rhyme or reason. Any company that's set up like that is not like one company with one decision maker. What people need to understand is that a big sale is an accumulation of a lot of little sales.

Some people we train tell me, "Well, that's not really the way my sales work. When I go into a big account, I go into the central buying office to see the purchasing agent or the CIO or the telecom manager. It's an enterprise sale and because I'm dealing with that person, I have access to the entire company—all the possible quadrants that could buy something at Proctor & Gamble or Federal Express or Coca-Cola—they have to buy from me. That's what my major account sale looks like."

So let's say the headquarters of that huge company was my existing account, and let's say that I'm trying to grow that account. Of course, the headquarters is one site, but they've got another division here and a couple of companies there and another company here and still another one over there.

Here's the tricky part. No matter what product I sell, even if they sign a contract with me, if I am supposedly the only vendor they can use to buy that product or service, there are going to be gaps in the coverage. In other words, not everybody is going to be buying from you, even though you might think they are, or should!

Here's how you can confirm that for yourself. If you happen to venture into the actual divisions or locations—I mean physically make a tour to actually figure out what's going on in the account, here's what's going to happen. You'll be expecting to see your product on the shelves everywhere. And you won't see that.

You'll see somebody else's product or service. You won't expect to, because theoretically you're the only company with the right to sell into the account. But you will in fact see somebody else's stuff there.

Supposedly, everybody's using your product or service in this "enterprise sale," but you will learn they're either not buying anything like what you sell, or, not infrequently, they have never even heard of what you sell. They know nothing about the contract that entitles you to exclusive access to every single desk in that operation. Lo and behold, there's a competitor in your enterprise sale, a competitor who has no right to be there!

What happened?

The thing we have to understand is this enterprise license isn't really a final judicial order that no other competitor can legally appear within that account that we consider ours. Instead, it's more like a hunting license. It gives us the opportunity to turn as much of that huge collection of potential sales into our customer base as we can. But we have to take the initiative.

All that hunting license gets you is the opportunity to go out and talk to people about how they can implement what you sell. These other areas may have totally different ways of thinking about whatever it is that you offer. You know what will happen when you remind them of your hunting license? They may say things like, "Well, we do it our own way," or "We have our own vendor arrangements," or "We have a legacy relationship that we maintain kind of quietly over here on the side." They may even say, "What enterprise contract?" or "Nobody told me we were supposed to change vendors." Or, "If I wanted, of course I could use you, but I have to go through the process of acquiring or buying it and I chose not to do that."

These are the kinds of things you're likely to hear when you actually get on the ground and figure out what's actually going on in your supposedly solid major account or key account where you supposedly have an enterprise arrangement or sole access to the market within that large organization.

A COMPANY IS A COLLECTION OF RIGHT PEOPLE

Our working principle is pretty simple: A company is a collection of right people. What we're trying to identify is as many right people as possible.

A lot of salespeople I work with go through this very complicated mapping process for major accounts. They ask the salesperson to picture an architect's drawing and fill in all the blanks with every conceivable decision maker. It can get very complicated. Rather than go through that, why not say, "Here are the opportunities within an account," and track each opportunity through the Prospect Management System?

These are all different people who could possibly either influence the bigger sale or get another piece of a sale. The sale I closed first is just one of those. Very often what I find is the enterprise solutions are first sold to the enterprise, but that is only the beginning. Even after I make it through headquarters, I have to be ready to set up a pilot program or deal over here, and with another one over there, and yet another one in this corner that is visible to everyone else in the organization, in order to get some meaningful chunk of the company to actually buy into the products and services that they are supposed to be buying enterprise-wide.

Believe it or not, we have to find a way to resell all the different "companies" we are dealing with. We cannot simply say that one deal, shake of the hand, or contract will instantly turn everyone in the organization into advocates of all products or services. That is just not the way it works. Things have to be customized, piloted, reintroduced, and re-networked throughout those huge (or even not so huge) organizations that we just sold under an enterprise agreement. In some major accounts, it is really something closer to 100 sales before you have the whole group.

38 THE HOLES IN THE DAM

Meanwhile, your competition does not know that they are supposed to stay away.

It's almost as though there were a dam with little holes breaking through at various times and at various points, and your job is to plug up each of the holes in the wall. That is a lot easier to do if you have allies throughout the organization, and if you have recruited other people to help you.

So how do I get those allies? I want to identify all the potential opportunities.

One of the things they do when they decide to buy for the first time is they provide for me, the seller, a centralized person who has been delegated or designated the task of being my contact. So, I might be tempted to think that I have to deal with that person and that person alone to get even more of a sale or to penetrate further. Maybe that person has the authority to keep buying what has been sold up to this point, but he or she may not have the authority to buy for other departments or divisions.

And, in fact, that is often the case. Even if our first contact did technically have the authority to pull that off, unless he or she gets the buy in from the other departments, our contact is probably not going to force anybody to do anything. Our contacts are going to need some kind of a consortium of support. I have to identify all the opportunities.

I am going to start by going to my contact and asking. "Who are the other departments and divisions and locations that might possibly be affected by what we are offering here?" At the end of that meeting, I'm going to say something like: "In fact, let me also do this. Can you and I go on a tour together, where we can actually see what is happening on the ground and meet some of these people?"

Let me give you an example from the real world of how this works. We sell sales training to office product companies, some of which have enterprise licenses with huge corporations. That huge company is supposed to buy, on an exclusive basis, all their office products from this one office products source. Guess what? They are not doing it! They are not in compliance with what Corporate thinks is happening.

If they had 100 percent total compliance, then they would be able to realize all of the savings that Corporate thought they were getting by working with a single vendor. We as salespeople have to try to plug up all of the holes in the dam. We have to identify all the opportunities, and we have to act as diplomats or advocates to reach out to the people within the organization who have decided, for whatever reason, that it does not yet make sense to work with us on enterprise level. There really is no single monolithic entity called "the company"—instead, we must assume that we're dealing with a huge collection of little companies.

Another thing to bear in mind is that companies are always changing. They are like big cities that way. They never stay the same even from one month to the next.

Even if we could somehow get 100 percent compliance at some point (which is impossible), it is quite likely that something would quickly slip. In addition, we would have new people to deal with, new entrants into the system who we are going to have to bring up to speed on the best ways to procure, learn about, and implement our solution.

Let's identify all of the opportunities now. Let's say to ourselves that we now take a big company and we have to identify all the people who could possibly buy. Let's say that there are 100 people. How would we want to track them?

A version of this question would play out if, for example, we were selling cell phones to that large company. I want the company to exclusively use my cell phones. So, I have to recognize that every different department has some kind of influence over the cell phones that are actually given to their employees. So the questions are:

- How many employees are there?

- How many total possibilities for cell phone usage are there in that group of employees?

- Who do those people report to?

- Who are likely to be the most influential decision makers?

- What is the dollar value of each of those subaccounts within the organization?

Another thing I have to do is find out what I actually know about these groups. Maybe I have to do some research and find out by talking to people or doing any other kinds of conventional research to learn about those people who could influence the purchase of cell phones within that organization.

With the help of my initial contact, and any other contacts I can pick up along the way, I'm going to build a network of allies. Each new opportunity that turns into a First Appointment with one of those allies is going to be tracked separately in the Prospect Management System.

Initially on my prospect management board, the opportunity column is going to show a lot of people for me to talk to. I am going to have to reach out in a sustained way, over a protracted period of time. That is where we start putting the two pieces together. If I do not have any appointments here, then I really have nothing else going within that organization and nothing happening within that account. I have to ask myself, out of all of those opportunities that I have at this organization, how many are actually turning into appointments?

By the way, the same approach works for distributors who have a connection to a single huge company. You'll want to win the same kind of allies, build the same kind of referrals, arrange the same kinds of meetings, and work patiently through all the various corners of the universe that does distribution for that big company. Throughout any kind of effort like this, you're going to identify selling opportunities, rank them within the Prospect Management System, and invest your time based on who's actually playing ball with you.

39 REACHING OUT TO NEW MAJOR ACCOUNTS

You want to know about a time when it pays to be really, really good at appointment making? It's when there's only a limited number of CFOs in a given industry, and you have to talk to all the major companies in that industry, and you have to reach out to each and every CFO.

We've actually trained people whose job is to sell like that. Their prospect base is the CFOs of the Fortune 500 companies. That means they have a total universe of 100 to 500 prospects! Obviously, they can't upset anybody, which is actually a pretty constructive dynamic, and they can't just say, "Oh, just go to the next call," if the call didn't go well! My dial-to-completed-call ratio has got to be much better on those kinds of sales calls than if I was just calling people blind out of the phonebook!

Here's what we've trained people in that situation to do. First, they know that they're going to have to be creatively, politely persistent with the call. That means they (a) have to pick times to call when they're likely to reach the top person, such as 6:30 p.m. or 7:00 a.m., and (b) they have to keep calling the same person, with exquisite tact, every two weeks or so. They can't afford to just say, "That lead is now dead."

What's more, they will build the call itself around ideas that are likely to be of instant interest to C-level decision makers. This is basically a call that says, "Mr. CEO, I believe that there's a possibility I could help you (make X dollars/save X dollars/save your people approximately X amount of time), because that's what we did for some of our other customers." (You can only pick one of those three things to focus the call on.) The call continues like this: "Let me show you some of the research I have done that suggests to me that there's a possibility we may be able to do this for you. Let me give you some examples of similar companies that we have worked with, so I can show you why I believe I could help you. Can I meet with you tomorrow morning at 8:00 A.M.?"

That's basically the call we have developed for people. There are also several turnarounds to use that help get past the runaround the CFO is likely to give you when you make that call. These turnarounds have to be pretty heavily customized, but basically they sound like, "That's exactly what your colleagues in the so-and-so industry thought before they had the chance to see how their priorities weren't really percolating through the organization. They ended up deciding that it was worthwhile to meet with me personally, and now they're really glad they did. Can we get together tomorrow morning at 8:00 A.M.?"

40 SELLING AT C-LEVEL

Once they get in the door, the overall message of that (typically very short) meeting is, in essence "My best guess is I could save your company approximately $1,000,000 a year." What we say is going to have to be that just about that stark and that direct. Here's the catch: you are going to have to be willing to stand by what you claim and then deliver on it! (That should go without saying, but I want to reiterate it anyway.)

When we make that bold statement to the CFO, what we have to do is phrase it like this, "By the way, some of the other companies I've worked with have reported X, Y, and Z as problems. Has that been your experience, too? I thought so. All right, well, based on that, yes, I think I can save you roughly $1,000,000 in the fiscal year X, based on the fact that we've worked with similar companies in similar situations. But, and this is a big but, I need to check my assumptions."

This is actually a very shrewd thing to say at this point, because any C-level decision maker worth his salt is going to be looking at that claim to save the company money with a certain degree of skepticism. So when we say, "That is what I think I can do but, I am going to check my assumptions to make sure that is the case," that's when the CFO actually starts to buy in.

We continue by saying, "Let me identify the people I am going to meet with to test these assumptions. It seems to me I am going to have to meet with the people in A department, B department, C department, and D department. Does that seem right to you?"

We will get by on that or be corrected one way or another. Then we are going to continue by saying something along the following lines: "What I am going to do is spend some time talking to these people, touring the facilities, auditing the process you currently have in place, and doing whatever analysis of that process I need to do. Then I am going to come back to you or to the people on your team with my final analysis, two weeks from today, at 10:00 A.M. Agreed?" In other words, we are offering to do the research in exchange for the commitment to be able to meet with this person again and show off the results of all that work we have done. It's a pretty good trade. We are basically offering free consulting for access.

That is the kind of exchange that a C-level decision maker will understand intuitively and be receptive to. And by the way, we do want to make it clear that we are making this investment because we want to get a decision from the C-level person or someone who reports directly to him. We are also going to say something like the following: "If my work turns out to point in the direction I think it is going to end up pointing, will you switch to me?" We really have to be that direct about it.

I guess a lot of salespeople who hear that advice are scared about asking a question that boldly: "Would you do business with me if I can save your company money and I can prove it to you?" The truth of the matter is you really do have to get that bold when you are stepping into the batting cage with a C-level decision maker. You really will not get any negative feedback for asking that question. As a matter of fact, you will often lose credibility if you fail to ask a direct question like that. After all, why go through what I have just outlined, namely meeting with all these different department heads and developing this elaborate defense of your analysis, if you do not get the opportunity to present it to the person who can actually implement it?

It is possible the CFO is going to tell you "Yes, $1,000,000 would be about right for us to switch vendors." Great! Now you know exactly what you have to do. What else could happen? If you get a negative answer, it's going to come in one of two forms. First, you could get, "Don't waste your time, I will never implement this under any circumstances." Well, wouldn't you rather know that now than six weeks from now? Second, and more likely in my view, is that the C-level contact says, "Actually, for $1,000,000 we would not switch vendors, but for $1,500,000.00, we would!" Now you know what the target is. Now you've got something to work toward over the next two weeks.

It's possible, of course, that over that two-week period, you may conclude that you can't deliver what you're forecasting. Be up-front about it. Talk honestly about what you've discovered. Come up with a Next Step that matches your real-world capabilities. Throw out the ball. See what happens. Just remember that any recommendation you make to this person must demonstrate that you have done the work and put in your due diligence. Once the C-level person at this account knows that, your recommendations will be taken a lot more seriously.

MORE THOUGHTS ON MAJOR ACCOUNT SELLING

Here are some additional thoughts on major account selling.

- Keep an eye out for ways to make your contact look good within his corner of the company.

- Make sure what you're suggesting is something he identifies as publicly valuable, not just your estimate of what will make the person look like a hero. (See Part Four for advice on effective interviewing on both the personal and the organizational level.)

- Because major accounts tend to have a pretty long sales cycle, you must begin new account prospecting regularly. For most of the people we train, we determine that prospecting for new business every month is a good target.

- Everyone you meet this year could be a decision maker in a different role within the company or with a different company next year. Stay in touch with everyone. Treat everyone as a future potential decision maker or influencer.

- Don't burn bridges.

- Ask everyone you meet for referrals.

- Don't assume the prospect's (stated) needs will necessarily result in sales. They may say they need you yet stay with someone else because that vendor has a better sense of the internal politics and/ or the buying cycle.

- Remember, fast changes are rare in major accounts. Not unheard of, but rare.

- Take time to learn about their buying process. It's usually every bit as important as the technical specifications of what you're selling, and sometimes considerably more important.

- Become a partner with your contacts. Work with them to meet their key players and learn their important goals. Introduce them to your key players and your important goals.

- Does the company have an appetite for additional product? Can they absorb the added purchase?

PART

THE RIGHT RELATIONSHIPS, THE RIGHT INFORMATION

ON "PUSHINESS"

Sometimes, when I am training on the topic of improving interviewing skills, and I make a suggestion about a way to ask a question or conduct a meeting or ask for a Next Step, people will stop my presentation and say, "You know, Steve, this isn't New York. You can't do that here. We don't sell the same way as in New York."

I always wonder what they mean. What would the theory be? That within the geographical confines of New York City, prospects want you to sell in some kind of aggressive or pushy way? That's the implication!

I think what happens is that you challenge somebody to be proactive, rather than reactive, and they then categorize that as "pushy," when in fact it's not pushy at all. It's simply what a professional salesperson does.

Yet salespeople are eager to assume that whatever I have just suggested to them is somehow a lapse of etiquette or a breach of manners everywhere except New York City. Actually, I think any salesperson has the right to try to take a certain amount of initiative within the conversation. I think doing so is nothing to apologize for, whether you're in New York City or somewhere else.

We want to be polite; we want to be respectful; we want to know when we should disengage, but we do not want to be passive. Bear in mind that what I am going to be proposing to you in the following chapters is actually not pushy selling. It is just intelligent selling. It's selling that knows what constitutes forward movement in a sales process, what doesn't, and choosing the former. You know what the real definition of being pushy in the sales process is? Pushy is when the salesperson really does not recognize that the person they are talking to simply is not interested in something, but keeps pushing the same idea anyway. That's pushy!

The whole secret of selling is trying to accurately gauge the person's level of interest, and then acting consultatively based on that. What we want to do is bring that interest along and develop it. We also want to recognize when the other person really does not want to go with us to the Next Step, and figure out that that's happening so we can find out what the problem is before we invest any more time and energy in the process.

It is much better to know what's really happening, even if you have to ask a direct question to figure that out, than it is keep on acting as though hints have not been dropped.

The really "pushy" salespeople are the ones who are oblivious. On the other hand, salespeople who ask the right questions, wait for the answers, and then look for ways to improve the relationship are the ones who make inroads in their key accounts.

LOOKING AT IT FROM BOTH SIDES

We are going to look now at two issues. First, how do we strategize the best way to expand and improve our relationship with this customer and get to the Next Step. Second, how do we recognize when that really is not as likely to happen as we might want, and what to do then.

The reason I have to look at this from both sides is that we want to minimize the amount of time that we waste with initiatives that ultimately are not going to turn into revenue for us. We really do not want to spend any more time than we absolutely have to trying to "sell uphill."

Think back to our definition of closing, as it applies to any one of your key accounts, or to any customer you would like to turn into a key account. There is absolutely no way you can force your contact into taking on any initiative that really does not make sense to him or her. So why try?

The critical point to understand is when it does make sense and what initiatives we have that match what the other person is trying to accomplish. This obviously is an art that takes many years to perfect, but there are some basic principles that that you can put to good use as you interact with your contacts.

Our goal is to avoid discussions that end up sounding like this:

"Hi, Mr. Customer. About a month or two ago I gave you a proposal, which, at that time, you said you had to think about. I guess the purpose of my call today is, well, to see if you've finished thinking about it, and have decided to buy from me, but haven't had time to get back to me."

That's the call we want to do anything to avoid making. Of course, that is not actually what we say, but isn't that basically what those follow-up calls sound like? When you get a salesperson calling you to say, "I'm just calling to follow up on . . .", what's your reaction? The fact that I am making a follow-up call in the first place, and announcing it as such, suggests that things are not going forward with the sale. Speaking personally, in this situation I'd be much more likely to send the customer a relevant book or article in the mail, then call to see what he or she thought of what I'd sent. Inevitably, the person apologizes for not having gotten back to me on the proposal, tells me what's going on, and suddenly we've got a discussion. I don't have to waste time and energy with the inevitable awkwardness of the whole "just following-up" opening.

NOT JUST ANY NEXT STEP

So we're trying to find ways to avoid that awkward dynamic where we're thinking things are moving forward, and acting as though they are moving forward, but the other person really isn't moving forward.

If you look at the sales process as we do, as a series of steps, the basic concept, as you know, simply says that our objective is to get to the Next Step. But that is not all there is to the picture, though. It is more than that. As you may have gathered by now, the objective of each step is really to see if the customer will agree to the Next Step that makes sense in order for the sale to move forward.

That is, we want them to agree, to not just any Next Step ("Can I call you next week?" "Sure!") but to one of the smaller subgroups of all possible Next Steps that could actually result in forward movement in the sale. Again, we have to be constantly asking ourselves, "What is the very next thing that I need to make happen in order for this sale to close, and is this person willing to do that with me?"

Here's an equally futile dialogue, which matches the pointlessness of the just following-up phone call:

> "Can I e-mail you a proposal?"
> "Sure, go ahead, send a proposal. I'll take a look at it and then I'll let you know how I feel about it."

Why shouldn't they agree to that? They are not investing anything, and we suggested a course of action that doesn't require them to invest in anything! Unless what I'm suggesting involves some kind of parallel effort on the part of the other person or on the part of my contact within the key account, I am not getting the kind of Next Step that I am looking for. I may not be able to close it at the next meeting, but what is the very next thing I want to do in order to try and close this sale? And how does this person fit into that? E-mailing the person does just about nothing on that score.

Sometimes people talk about "buying signals" during the interview. What about not-buying signals? Not-buying signals would be a more relevant thing to watch out for. After all, the majority of the things you put together do not turn into income.

Let's look more closely at some of the not-buying signals that may show up when we're interacting with one of our key accounts.

WHAT USUALLY HAPPENS?

A not-buying signal is something that usually indicates the person is not moving forward with us. To put it a more colorful way, a not-buying signal is a (purported) prospect displaying anything that I would call *hair*.

What do I mean by that word, *hair*?

Assume you've got a story to your sales process that sounds like this: "I'm going back tomorrow at 10:00 A.M. for a second meeting."

Or: "The contact agreed to meet with me again next Tuesday and I still want to find out some more about the structure of his division."

Well, that's a very smooth second meeting. It's a classic way for the second meeting about this project to move forward.

Or if I ask you about one of your key accounts, and you tell me, "Tomorrow I'm expecting the purchase order; they said they'd fax it in the morning." That, too, is a clean story.

Or even: "I called the contact and he agreed to let me take a tour of the plant. He wants me to meet a couple of people, and we're all going to sit down and see whether there's a match for more work there." That's very clean, too. There's no doubt whatsoever about what's happening.

But the problem is that other stories tend to grow hair sometimes, and then they are not always quite so clean. We've developed a slang phrase for any prospect story that depends on things that are totally out of the salesperson's control. We call that a sale with too much hair on it.

Sometime we ask people to say where exactly in the system they would categorize their key account prospects, the people they want to get continuing business from, and we hear people say things like this:

"Well, as long as this contact talks to this other contact, then I should be able to move forward; I'll know next Tuesday."

Or:

"I just e-mailed him, but he is very busy, so I should check in with him next week."

Or:

"I have to wait until this contact who I've never met comes back from Japan."

Or:

"It's looking good, but the whole company's going to Mars for a retreat and they're supposed to call me when they get back within 100,000 miles of Earth's orbit."

Any kind of strange convoluted story with lots of weird details that you have no control over is a sale with hair on it. Actually, it's not even a sale with hair on it, it's a fantasy with hair on it, because each and every one of these weird convoluted details is a not-buying signal. Those strange, inexplicable roadblocks that show up for no discernable reason—those are usually polite ways that the person has strategized to say no to you.

Not always. But usually. What usually happens is what we're trying to focus on.

The moment you have any kind of hair on your prospect, a good question to ask yourself is, am I waiting for them or are they waiting for me? If there is any kind of delay, if there is any question about anything that gets in the way of your having forward progress on the sale, that is a not-buying signal. Often, something may be happening that you're not aware of; perhaps the CFO has put all decisions on hold, for example.

When I run into one of these not-buying situations, I get face-to-face with my contact and say some variation on the following: "Usually, when I get to this stage with someone I really feel is a match, I get a better sense of where we are, and I'm really not sure where we are here. Did I do something wrong along the way?"

Not always, but usually, I'll get a clearer sense of what's happening in the account when I say that. Knowing what's going on is much better than not knowing what's going on. Asking my contact if I've made a mistake doesn't make me pushy. It makes me a more knowledgeable participant in the conversation.

46

IMPROVING COMMUNICATION, IMPROVING THE RELATIONSHIP

The number one thing you can do to improve communication between you and your primary contact is improve the relationship.

The better your relationship is with somebody, the more effective your communication is going to be. It seems self-evident, but putting that principle into practice can be a major challenge for everyone in sales.

Let's say you're talking on the phone to a person you've known for a long time. Suppose you're having a difficult conversation because you're telling him what you believe in your heart is helpful for him to know, but he hasn't quite signed on to the value of your message yet. Well, there's one thing that's good about that situation. At least you don't believe he's going to be happy hearing what you have to say!

As you're telling this person what you have to tell, assume there's a silence or a pause. As you go on with that discussion you can probably visualize the look on the person's face. You can imagine what he's thinking about. You might even be able to put together some mental image of what his posture might be. You can really picture the whole moment as you're relaying that painful or difficult message. And you know what? You'd be right.

Now compare that to a similar phone call that represents a conversation that you have with an important business contact you've met only two or three times. Let's say that you have something to say to this person that you think may be helpful to them, but may also be a little bit difficult to process. There's the same ten-second pause. This time around, you don't know if the phone went dead or if the person is holding the phone away from their ear, covering the mouthpiece and giggling in the background. You don't know if the person is scribbling a note to somebody else across the desk saying, "Get me a corned beef sandwich." You really don't know anything about the way this person is or is not interacting with your message.

Why? Because you don't have as meaningful a relationship with this person as you have with the person you've known for twenty years, and you have no reference for what their reaction to your message is going to be.

In fact, it's quite likely that the person is going to miss the whole thing even if they don't hold the phone away from their ear, because they may be simply focusing on something else. There are so many different stresses and so many different inputs when you have a conversation with somebody these days that you can't even be sure that you're the only thing on a person's mind. You really don't have any idea what kind of reaction or response is happening on the other end of the line.

My point is that improving your relationship helps you understand the other person's daily patterns of interaction, his or her vocabulary, and, ultimately gives you the ability to understand the filter through which this person is going to view you and your message.

So, improving the relationship really is the first and most important thing you can do to improve the communication. It's a long-term process, yes, but that makes it more important, not less. In the next chapters, we'll start looking at some strategies for improving the communication with your key account contacts.

THE MOST OBVIOUS IMPROVEMENT

One thing you can do to improve the communication seems obvious, but it nevertheless eludes a lot of salespeople. Do your best to make sure that at all times the conversation is genuinely interesting to the other person.

I know. It sounds like the sort of thing that salespeople would automatically do anyway. But I have to tell you that after having not only trained out on sales meetings with thousands of professional salespeople over the years, my experience is that it's quite rare that a person actually takes the time, effort, and energy necessary to make sure the conversation really is interesting to the prospect. It's one of our professional responsibilities; most sales managers and customers would agree that it's an area that salespeople don't succeed in all the time.

Most salespeople are very good at focusing on what they're interested in, which is usually what they're best at talking about. Typically, that's their own products and services. But, sometimes they're less skilled at connecting with the values and issues that are of greatest importance to the *prospect* or *customer.*

So what's the most interesting thing to me? What's the most important thing to me? What I do. That's my topic. If we build the whole conversation around what the customer does, what goals the customer had prior to the meeting, and what happened immediately before the meeting, we're going to be a lot better off.

Think of the sales meeting as a kind of movie. If you were an actor playing in a movie and you were engaged in the research necessary to do that scene properly you'd want to know what had happened immediately before the scene began The same thing goes with a professional sales conversation. To make sure what we're saying is relevant and interesting, we have the similar responsibility to find out what happened right before we walked in the door. We should come up with a theory about what we think is right, evaluate whether that theory is correct, and try to work with the prospect to find out what exactly happened.

Think about it. The prospect had a life before you walked in the door, right? He had goals, time lines, pressures, meetings, and all sorts of things happening. In fact, the quality of the meeting is going to be affected by the specific events that took place right before our meeting or discussion happens. What big picture agenda item was being dealt with right before you walked in? How did it affect the company, and department? These are questions you may not always be able to get a complete and clear answer to. You should be able to have a working theory, though, and then see how close you were as the meeting unfolds.

This is important because we have to keep tying our sale to whatever that big agenda item is. That's what's most interesting to the people we're talking to. It's their own number one item on the agenda. We have to attempt to understand what was on the agenda before we started the discussion, and we have to keep finding creative ways to ask about whether we're on the right track or not. That's the only way we're going to match up what we are offering with what they are trying to do.

48 SPEAK THEIR LANGUAGE

To improve our communication with prospects, we have to speak their language. What do I mean by that? I'm not talking about the dictionary definition of *language*, I'm talking about trying to get some sense of their business language, the terms that make a lot of difference in their world that really don't come up in our discussions with other prospects and customers.

We don't have to memorize every single technical term that may come up. Yes, we want to make sure we're making an effort to complement the other person's verbal sophistication. It will take a couple of meetings to get the balance right perhaps, but this will be time very well spent.

Above all, avoid inserting your company's jargon into discussions with people who have no reason whatsoever to recognize it. The minute you start using words that somebody doesn't understand, or that aren't appropriate to the other person's world or that person's industry, there's going to be a disconnect. (A similar disconnect will ensue if you misuse the other person's terminology. This is, alas, fairly easy to do, especially in the early going. What can I tell you—it's a matter of trial and error.)

We also want to match the communication style of the person we're dealing with. If we're talking to somebody who's primarily visual, we're going to use lots of imagery, ask them to picture such-and-such an idea, match their speed and intensity, and show them visual displays at any and every opportunity. For other people, we're going to focus on feelings, reactions, emotions, and relationship consequences. We're also going to slow down the tempo a little bit. Finally, we're also going to run into people who are essentially auditory. These are people who really need to *hear* the message, and not only that, they need to hear it a little more slowly than the way we'd talk to a visual person, and a little more rapidly than the way we'd talk to a person more oriented towards feelings. For these people, we want to emphasize concepts of listening and hearing things out.

Not everyone falls neatly into one of these three groups, but most people have one style that dominates. Make a practice of trying to classify your contacts in your key account base against these criteria, and of matching your communication style to theirs. If you do it right, you will instantly and powerfully connect with the person.

49

USE PROPS

The next thing I'm going to do to improve communication with my key accounts is to use props. By props I mean not only visual aids like flipcharts, summaries, and PowerPoints, but also every kind of sample, recommendation, endorsement, or write-up on my company I can find. The more relevant stuff my contacts have to look at during the meeting the better off I am going to be.

When I'm dealing with a primarily visual communicator, my strong tendency is to use some kind of visual to demonstrate what I'm doing if it's at all possible. I'm going to use visual aids during the meeting to drive the sale forward. (Not everybody I talk to is going to be primarily a visual communicator, but even those people who are not visually driven, are likely to react positively to a well-designed flow chart or visually driven summary.)

Props help bring a meeting alive in a way that's simply impossible if you're simply talking. If you're not comfortable or familiar with PowerPoint shows, of course, there's always the tried and true "let me show you what I mean," maneuver, which simply involves drawing a picture to illustrate what you're talking about.

That's a great way to engage the person and get him to connect with you. If all else fails, use your yellow legal pad as a prop. (I discuss the importance of taking notes during meetings with prospects and customers in more depth in Chapter 64.)

Whenever we go a sales meeting with somebody for a second or third time, we always come with a large laminated kind of overview sheet that displays all of the information that is contained in our multipage written document. In other words it serves as kind of a visual reference point and an easy-to-interpret visual overview of what we think the meeting ought to look like. The agenda should take the form of one big flowchart, driven by arrows and rectangles. It's basically a cartoon that can help the person get to the point where they say, "I've got it."

50

UNDERSTAND THE THREE UNIVERSAL PRINCIPLES

There are three universal principles that will help us communicate with prospects in our key accounts. We should diligently study and internalize all three.

The first principle has two parts: Principle 1-A and Principle 1-B. Principle 1-A reads as follows: **People respond in kind.** Its corollary is the same idea, just expressed from a different perspective: Principle 1-B says, **We control the flow.**

Suppose I were to look at you, smile admiringly, and say, "You look *great*. What's your secret?"

Well, that question, that tonality, and that emotion would have a certain effect on you, and would elicit a certain response from you. The words I chose to say would encourage you to respond in kind to the specific question (and its assumptions) that I posed. If you're like most people, there's a good chance that you would start telling me what your secret was and find a reason to feel great about the day, even if you didn't have one before I asked.

Suppose, though, that, instead of saying that to you, I were to stare at you in horror, frown, lean over confidentially and whisper the following words in your ear: "You look terrible. What happened?"

Again, that question, that tonality, and that emotion would have a predictable effect on the conversation, and what I said would elicit a particular response. You would respond in kind to what I had said, and would respond accordingly. It would be a completely different conversation (and probably a considerably less pleasant one).

I have a choice when it comes to how I begin the conversation. That means I, as the questioner (and effective salespeople are, in my view, effective questioners) *control the* flow. I can choose the questions I pose, and move the conversation in a particular direction by the topics I raise. That's not to say that I can script the interview, of course, but I can navigate, to a certain extent, by planning the direction of any question or sequence of questions.

Now, let's look at the second principle. It reads as follows: ***All responses can be anticipated.*** That means that I, as a salesperson, usually have more experience at dealing with responses, positive or negative, than any given sales prospect has in dishing them out to me. To give you a very quick thumbnail of this principle, consider the customer at a key account who strings you along for a few weeks, sends you nothing but positive signals, and then suddenly tells you that things are on hold, without giving you any meaningful information as to why. Well, this may be unfortunate, but it's hardly unpredictable. This kind of thing has probably happened to you before, which means that you've got a head start on a good strategy for dealing with just this kind of situation, based on your own past experience. You might say, for instance, "I have to tell you, I'm really surprised to hear you say that, because typically, when we get this far into the process, people I've worked with are really pretty eager to move forward. Did I miss something? Why are things on hold?" If that doesn't succeed in getting the needed information, you would probably still have plenty of experience in dealing with that situation, and you could still anticipate what should happen next. You might ask a colleague or your boss to call the person after you have left and say, "Listen, I understand there was a problem. Did Joe Salesperson do something wrong?" At that point, I can pretty much guarantee, you will find out what's really happening in the account. Nine times out of ten, your contact will give that person a reality-based summary of what's actually happened to make things stop cold.

How about the third principle? It sounds like this: **People communicate through stories.** It isn't really a relationship until one of the parties shares a story with the other party that changes how that person looks at something. Now, this principle works in two directions. We should be ready to share relevant success stories with every single person we sell to. We're going to get people to relate to what we're talking about because we're going to give them examples of others like them who have used our products to solve similar challenges. Those stories will help people to visualize what's going on, and what *could* be going on, in the relationship.

By the same token, we should seek to elicit stories from everyone within the key account who has any kind of role to play in the decision making process. That means our primary contact, the formal decision makers, and the influencers who affect the sale. If each and every one of those people has had a good enough discussion with us to share a meaningful story (about how the company has solved problems like this in the past, for example) we will improve the quality of the relationship.

I've given you just a brief overview of these three universal communication principles, and you can see how each one of them carries huge implications as you work to improve your communication with the people in your client base. Study the three principles. Memorize them. Use them!

■ ■ ■

So my first sales strategy within my key account base is to improve the relationship and improve the communication. Doing so helps me figure out what they're going to DO, and that really is what it is all about. The whole reason I'm focusing on this problem of improving the communication is that I want to have a higher likelihood of having the person actually share meaningful information with me. I want to know what they're trying to accomplish, how they're trying to accomplish it, who the key people are who are trying to get it accomplished, and how my product or service might fit in with that. That's our job as salespeople, figuring all that stuff out.

Let's take a closer look at the dynamics of that job now.

UNDERSTAND THE PRESSURES ABOVE AND BELOW THE PLANE

When we're working with an individual and moving through the four steps of the process with him, going from step to step to step, there are pressures both above and below that decision-making plane that can affect our sale.

I know as you're reading this you probably can think of examples of what I'm talking about, with somebody perhaps below the level of your decision maker—say, an Influencer. This is someone who can't make the decision, but who can find some way to block the sale, somebody who actually uses a competing product and who has, for whatever reason, a good relationship with that other vendor. Those kinds of people can find a way to make your sale not happen even though they have may have, technically, lower status and authority than the person you're talking to.

By the same token, it's quite possible that somebody with a higher status—say the CEO of the organization—can freeze everything in place, and then intervene and change the rules. So maybe at the end of the process you're a lot further away from closing the sale than you appeared to be before the CEO intervened.

This same process might play out with the partner of a law firm or any high-ranking person in the organization. If they have customers who push back with a certain decision or other key constituents whom they have to keep happy, it's going to be quite common for somebody above your contact's level to intervene and find a different way for the sale to conclude. As salespeople we have to first of all recognize that there are informal and formal influences that affect our selling cycles. We really have to understand who each of these people is dealing with, who our contacts are dealing with, and who their internal constituents are.

We have to work with our primary contact to get to the other people. I'm not saying you should go over our contact's head or undermine her, but you should first and foremost make the effort to work with her to get to all the other people in the organization.

Right now, we're concerned with how to reach out to those other players within the organization in a face-to-face mode. (Phone contact is covered in Chapter 9.)

Who should our primary contact be? What title should that person have? Who are the other people? To answer these questions, we have to understand where in the buying process the company is because that's going to affect the roles that people have. Sometimes a given contact really will be the right person—the person who could and will influence the decision that gets made. Sometimes, when there's a different dynamic in play, that same individual is not the right person, but may be an influencer.

How do you figure out what's going on? By identifying the three likely patterns that may be in play when it comes to a company approaching a purchase decision. I call these patterns the stages of the buying process, and anyone who hopes to sell to key accounts should really understand all three, and be able to identify which is in play at any given time.

IMPs

52

There are three places that customers can be in the buying process: *IMP, EMP,* or *CC.* This chapter is about the first of those groups.

To begin at the most obvious point, they could be ready to buy right now. We call those people **IMPs** for *In the Marketplace.*

They're ready to buy right now because they have five things in place.

They have an agenda. By this I mean only that they know *why* they're buying. They're not buying training, for example, to get training. They're not buying a phone system to get a phone system. They're buying a product or service because it has a place in some bigger picture and because this initiative solves some larger problem that they've been empowered to address. For example, you might buy training in order to gain a competitive edge, to energize your sales force, or to launch an exciting new product. There might be an overall initiative to make a company more competitive, make the people more productive, lower costs, improve margins, or make the company more attractive to investors. All of these things are initiatives that people who are in the marketplace for training may be trying to fulfill. That's what we call a big-picture agenda, and my contact is doing what he's doing, namely fulfilling that agenda, for a series of related but different reasons. Also, note that my contact has an individual agenda for implementing the company's agenda: this person usually wants to change the amount of work, power, status, or rewards that he receives. For that person, that's the big-picture agenda on the personal level. I have to know about both agendas! By the time the company is ready to buy they also have a budget. They know how much money they want to spend because they've been looking into it for a while.

Third, they also know the timetable. They know when they're going to buy.

The fourth thing they know is their buying criteria. At the IMP level, they know what it's going to look like, when they're going to buy it, what kind of vendor they're trying to track down, and so on.

The fifth thing that they have in place when a buyer is in the marketplace is a designated or delegated person, a contact, who will work with the supplying company. Let's say there's an employee in the company who is named Joe and who is the so-called "technical person." Joe may be a lower-level employee in the hierarchy of the company, but once the company goes ahead and says it's going to buy this technical product, they know what it looks like, they know roughly how much it's going to cost, they might well authorize Joe to spend up to X number of dollars to buy it. (Remember, Joe has an agenda, too, just like the company does.) At that point, any supplying company has to work with Joe. At that moment, Joe is a decision maker.

If you called up Joe thirty seconds after he was told "Joe, I want you to handle this," and you asked him, "Joe, are you the decision maker?" He would say, "Yes," and he *would* be the decision maker. He would be telling you the truth.

EMPs

Now, the day before Joe was told that he was supposed to handle this purchase, his company was still in search mode, but in a different, less active version of it.

At the point right before the company concluded for certain what it wanted to buy, what the reason was for buying it, how much money to spend, and all those other things, they were still looking into doing something. They just hadn't prioritized yet, and they hadn't figured out who was in charge of delivering those priorities.

That company is not an IMP (In the Marketplace) company. Instead, it is what we call an **EMP**, because it is *Entering the Marketplace*.

These people are looking, they're educating themselves, but they're missing at least one or more of those five elements that are on the IMP company's list. Something on that list of five things has yet to be finalized. Usually, they know why they're looking but they haven't yet settled on a budget or a timetable.

They typically don't know the buying criteria yet, although they may involve the same designated or delegated person at that point to help figure out what the buying criteria should be. But that person isn't quite yet the decision maker, although he is probably the lead person among those who are dealing with either current or prospective vendors.

How do potential customers educate themselves about what they want to buy? Well, like the rest of us, they probably hit the Internet, do a search, and maybe make a few calls to the current vendor. In that case, if we're the current vendor and it's our key account, they're probably going to call us.

However, we can't assume that the education process is going to stop with us. In fact, we have to assume they're going to invite other salespeople from other companies in, and we have to assume that those potential vendors are going to ask questions such as, "If you could change anything about your relationship with your current provider, what would you change?"

If we go on the assumption that's not going to happen, then we're going to be sadly mistaken. In fact, we don't even have to assume that there's an outgoing call from our customer. What's more likely to happen is that there's going to be a salesperson out there who happens to call one of your key accounts right at the point when they're in an EMP process about some new initiative. Maybe this initiative is something you know about, maybe it's something you don't know about. In any event, some competitor of yours is going to make a cold call, reach the contact and they're going to ask the contact whether or not he's interested in talking about working with a new company.

You know what's going to happen? The contact's going to invite that sales representative in for a meeting. He's going to say, "What a coincidence; we are in fact actually looking at acquiring just this sort of thing right now. I'd love to hear what you have to say about this." Even an Influencer who will have only a tangential role in the decision-making process may meet with your competition. In fact, it's going to be relatively easy for that person to meet, not only with your contact, but with people in the organization you've never heard of! Even though you may be a vendor with the account, when people are in the EMP mode, we have to operate under the assumption that they're talking to other people.

In this situation, Joe may tell you he's the decision maker, and may actually even think he is the decision maker, but he would be mistaken. There is no decision maker yet.

Mastering Your Key Accounts

The second mode, the EMP mode, is when the company is entering the marketplace. From our point of view, getting new business from someone we haven't worked with before is something we want to encourage. If it's our customer, we want to prevent our competitors from poaching on our territory. We want to keep the customer from reaching out to talk to other people or searching to find the right vendor for this new initiative if we can actually do the job ourselves. All the more important, then, that we get our contact to give us face-to-face introductions to all of those people—whether Influencers or eventual Decision Makers—who might end up having any kind of contact with the competition.

54 CCSs

There is a third category of people in the buying process, people who have turned to a particular vendor first, and perhaps exclusively. These folks view the entire buying process through the lens of a particular vendor (and, ideally, of course, that's us). We describe someone like this as a **CC**, for *Cloistered Customer*.

Cloistered means "surrounded by or enveloped by." This means the customers are "covered"; there really isn't any search happening. People are pretty satisfied with the relationship they've got with a given supplier, and while it's not impossible for them to switch to someone else, doing so isn't perceived as a priority. The incumbent vendor is what makes sense right now. That vendor is the status quo.

It's quite common for people you meet in this group to tell you that they are, in fact, the decision maker and that isn't the case. I urge you to ask these folks questions about when, how, and why the last similar decision was made. If the person has no idea whatsoever, you may be sure you are not dealing with a prospective decision maker for this purchase.

The actual distribution of these three groups of customers would look something like this:

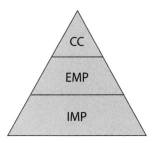

At the top of the triangle, at the CC level, there is a customer who's already working with us—and who's going to assume, by default, that if there's any education or any new initiative to discuss, they're going to work primarily and perhaps exclusively with us. So in that situation, we've built up enough goodwill. We've delivered enough profitable outcomes to that customer that we're "tops on the list." That's obviously where we want to be from the point of view of maintaining and protecting our work within the account.

Of course, we want to expand our base to reach new customers. We're on the lookout for people who are EMPs or IMPs and might buy from us for the first time. However, in terms of our people, ones I've already sold to, our goal is to just try to find out as much as we can about what they're doing. We need to get them at that CC level by developing a great dossier of information and customized proposals that generate repeat business within the account.

Most of the people in these three categories have a relationship with someone. This relationship might not be with us, but they have a close relationship with some vendor. It's just a question of how *strong* that relationship is.

Well, suppose it's *your* customer and *your* relationship. Is the relationship strong enough to stay in the CC category? How do you know?

55

YOUR CLOISTERED CUSTOMERS

You don't know it now, but tomorrow morning, your competition will be sitting down for a first meeting with your very best customer.

They had to turn around objections and get through voice mail and get the person to call back, and it took six weeks, and finally, tomorrow at 9:00 A.M., your competition is face-to-face with the person who signed your last purchase order.

What will happen?

Well, as we saw at the outset of this book, it's actually not that difficult to figure out how the meeting will open. What your competition is going to say will sound more or less like this: "What is it that you would change about your current supplier?" (Or: "What keeps you up at night?" Or: "Are you happy with your current supplier?")

By this point in the book, those questions should sound familiar to you. That's good. They *have* to be familiar to you, because, you will be in a terrible competitive position if your customer offers any variation on this answer: "Let me think. There's got to be something I don't like about working with them. Oh, yeah, I know. There was this thing six months ago . . ."

Similarly, you will be in a terrible competitive position if your customer says, "What would I change? What wouldn't I change? Here, take a look at my list of grievances."

You will be in a great competitive position if your customer instead offers a variation on this answer: "It's funny you should mention that. This is exactly the question my sales rep asked me when we had our monthly meeting. She said, 'What would you change about the way we're doing things here for you? Is there anything different we should be focusing on?' And then you know what happened? I came up with three or four issues, she took notes, and she solved them all. Every single one."

I've said it before, but I want to emphasize the point again, because it's incredibly important. Take the time and trouble to meet in person on a regular basis with your contacts at key accounts and ask them the same questions your competitors are likely to ask. Don't ask them about your competitor—ask them about your own company. No, you don't want to commit professional suicide here, but you should make sure you cover all the possible issues that a competitor would bring up during a meeting with your prospect.

Specifically, your questions for your customer should focus on your company's:

- Quality

- Timeliness

- Follow-through

- Ability to meet or exceed expectations

If you're in any doubt about the topics you should be addressing with your customer, take a good, long look at the bullet points that outlined the benefits you predicted in the last sales proposal you developed for this customer. Ask yourself: Did we deliver on this? Does the customer think so? If not, what can we do in the short term to improve the situation? What can we do in the long term? Then share your thoughts with your customer and ask for comments.

56 GETTING IT RIGHT

Sometimes when you meet with people at companies that you're trying to build more business with, you will hear them talk down a current supplier they're using. Customers will say, "You know, we're currently thinking about buying X from somebody like you. In fact, we were going to buy it from our existing supplier, but we really don't like them for reasons A, B, and C. In fact, we hate them."

Hearing something like "We hate them" usually produces the internal mental reaction on the part of the salesperson of "I've got the sale."

We start thinking like this: "Great! I'm going to get a sale! The sale is imminent! They don't like their existing supplier! They're going to change and they're going to buy from me!"

I've learned, however, that there's something that doesn't make sense in that equation. Because if they really hated the current supplier what would they already have done? They would have changed suppliers!

Maybe *hate* to them doesn't mean the same thing as *hate* to me. To me, *hate* means they would've changed. But look at the customer. Here he is in this relationship that he says isn't working for him, and yet he's sticking with it.

What's going on? Well, maybe the person's exaggerating in order to get you to invest time and energy in the discussion. (That's certainly not out of the realm of possibility.)

Or maybe that particular person really does hate what's happening in this relationship with the current vendor, but somebody else in the organization really likes the current vendor. Or, maybe "hate" isn't the real issue. For example, look at a copier salesperson.

The copier salesperson may begin the discussion with a question like, "Are you happy with your copier right now?" Well, think about that question for a minute. How happy could you be with a copier? With most copiers, it's kind of a maintenance relationship. As long as there's nothing disastrously wrong, I don't hate it, I can work with it. With my copier, as long as I'm not thinking about the copier, I figure that's about as good as it's ever going to get. I'm not thinking about the copier: that's the victory.

 If something happened and I did hate it, and I was the decision maker, I'd go out and get a new one if it mattered that much to me.

Sometimes my referral within a key account of mine will point me toward an opportunity for new business within his company. Sometimes, that new contact will give me suspiciously positive-sounding phrases such as, "We hate the current supplier," or "We're all ready to buy," or "I'm so glad Tom referred you to me." Whenever I hear something like that, I ask, "I'm just curious, had Tom not put the two of us in touch with each other, what were you going to do?"

When I ask that, I'm listening for one thing: "took action" versus "took no action." Those two categories of response are very different, and they're going to tell me a whole lot about the situation I'm walking into.

Here's what a "took action" response sounds like: "I called the ABC Company and they're coming in tomorrow."

Here's what "took no action" sounds like: "I was going to call the ABC Company."

If they did call somebody, I'll ask who. They sometimes, but not always, will mention the names. Even if I don't get the name, I'll continue the questioning in a way by asking, "Okay, I understand that you don't want to share that with me, but just out of curiosity why did you choose that vendor? What in particular made them an appealing choice for you?"

This "Why them" choice reveals their buying criteria, which is a big issue for me.

I might also ask, "I'm just curious, if you did look in this area before, I'm wondering why you didn't contact us," or "Did you even think of contacting us?"

Other questions I might ask such a person include:

- "How did you make the decision last time around?"

- "Why did you make the decision in the way you did?"

- "How long have you been with that other supplier?"

By the way, if there really is a problem now, I want to be sure I understand exactly why there's a problem. Things must been fine for that customer at one point. If suddenly they're very unhappy with it, the big question I want answered is: Why? Something must have changed. There are four broad possibilities to look at here.

- Something has changed for the customer

- Something's going to change for the customer

- Something has changed with the supplier

- Something is about to change with the supplier

Whatever it is, it has to fall into one of those four categories. For example, consider cell phone companies. The customer calls up and says, "My cell phone bills are so high! That's not what I thought was going to happen when I signed up a year ago."

What changed? Either the cell phone company changed their rates, or more likely, the customer is using the phone in a different way than they originally thought they were going to. Okay, what would you use a cell phone for, if you were a businessperson? You might use it to talk to customers, suppliers, prospects, and business partners. If you're talking to those people, those are all good signs. But you might need a new plan, one that matches up better with what's changed recently in your world.

All of these questions are designed to help us guess well when we have to determine about whether the company is in IMP mode (taking action), EMP mode (considering taking action) or CC mode (unlikely to consider taking action unless persuaded by a compelling case).

If we guess wrong about which category the person falls into, we tend to pace our sale or do things that we think would match up with where we think the customer should be in the buying process.

If we what we think is happening in the buying process is that the person is ready to buy, and we convince ourselves that we don't want to miss out on this imminent sale, you know what we do? We rush a proposal to them. The problem is, we may be dealing with an Influencer on the sale, and we may have no contact whatsoever with the eventual decision maker.

If, on the other hand, our meeting is with somebody who is not looking, thinking, or considering buying what I'm selling, and if I learn that early on, I know that they're not going to make a decision so fast. Then I do a different thing. I get more information and I work on my relationship.

How much information gathering I do, how I pace the sale out or how I don't pace it out, and at what point in the sale I rush that proposal or don't rush the proposal—these are all strategic decisions. When I decide to contact the other people in the company and when I don't hinges on where I think they are in the buying process. With EMPs and CCs, my priority is to get new contacts going. With IMPs, my priority is to engage with the real decision makers and get the most competitive proposal with verified information into their hands as quickly as I can.

My diagnosis about the company's position in the buying process is absolutely critical for another reason. It determines who I'm going to try to reach.

If the company is cloistered, then the chances are good that I need to reach out to somebody who's a very high-level person in the organization, typically a CEO or CFO, because they're the people who are going to delegate or designate an eventual contact. They're really the only people who can put together a constituency for change if there's already a strong commitment to an existing buyer.

If I get closer to the EMP company, I probably don't need to incorporate that high-level contact within the discussion. What I want to do is find the person who is likely to be delegated as the contact person within that organization. I'm trying to identify the person who is going to be given the responsibility of selecting the vendor. Somebody is going to take the lead, even if there's a committee in play. Now, identifying that individual who will emerge and take the lead may be a tricky operation, but it's something that's going to be important enough to build up an ever-larger network of contacts within the account.

Of course, in the IMP situation, I'm going to look for the person who actually has been delegated with the authority to make the purchase. In this situation, we've already defined that there really is likely to be only one person, or at least a trend toward dealing with one person. In the EMP scenario, there are still going to be a number of candidates in play for that role.

MOVING TOWARD RESOURCE

How do I get from my contact to the other people? What happens if I get in and I find out that I have to contact a different person or even more than one person at a time? What if I'm dealing with an EMP situation, and there's more than one right person to talk to? (That's very commonly the case when you're in an EMP situation.)

To answer these questions, I have to give you an overview of the four places that your relationship with a customer can be. Here are the four stages:

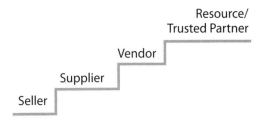

Notice that the steps rise as the quality of the relationship improves.

Sometimes during training programs, I will share this model with salespeople who are responsible for generating revenue from key accounts. Then I'll ask a question, "How many people will consider their relationship with their number one key account to be at the partnership, or resource level?" Most people will raise their hand. Then I'll pick someone from the group, and I'll say, "That's great. How many people do you know at that company?"

There will be an uncomfortable little pause.

"Well, right now I only know one person."

Then I'll ask, "Could you set up a meeting this week with your primary contact and his boss if you absolutely had to do that?"

Then there's another uncomfortable little pause.

"Well, no, but...."

Then I shake my head. I say, "I'm sorry, but that's not a partnership relationship. If you were truly a resource, you'd have that kind of access."

That's how I know whether or not something is at the partnership level in my world: I have access to all the people I need to talk to and I have access to the all the information I need. There is nothing off limits in this relationship. Once I make a connection with somebody at the CFO or CEO level or the owner of the company and they know that a strategic partnership has evolved over the months or years that we have been working together, I'm an insider! Not only do I have access, but that top-level person at that organization makes absolutely certain that I have regular updates on issues that are of importance to both his company and mine. In fact, they are going to go out of their way and say, "Here is a heads-up about something important. You should know about this."

We know all their key players, and they know all ours. Why? We are mutually interdependent.

That's where we want to be. That's the direction we want to go. However, this kind of high-access, high-information relationship emerges over time, and, speaking realistically, it's not going to be something you'll see happen with every customer. How do you get there and what should you know about expanding your contact base if you're in one of the earlier three steps?

Let's look at the level right before the partnership or resource level. At this third level, the **Vendor** level, you have a good-news/bad-news thing going. The good news is that you have an ongoing relationship, and you and your contact know each other very well. At this stage, you and your company have become the status quo. It is easier for them to stay with you than to leave.

Here's the bad news. Your point of contact has been reduced down to that one person. If you have been selling to them for twenty years, they have been buying from you for twenty years, and you know everything there is to know about each other on a social level but you only know that one person. If you basically only know him or her on a social level, then you are extremely vulnerable competitively.

In that situation, you really are not getting everything you need to out of the relationship and more often than not you are not even moving toward getting to that resource level.

Now, we've already established many times a key account sale hinges on our ability to take our product and service and bend it, shape it, and adapt it to what the company is going to do. Not just what it is doing right now, but what it plans to do in the future. If our contact either does not know that or does not share it with us, and we get stuck at that third level, then we are still vulnerable even though we are the status quo.

So our course is clear: We've got to find a way to learn more about this person's working world, and the people who affect it.

That means two things. First, we have to get ready for a potentially long period of time to pass while we make continuous, patient attempts to move from the Vendor level to the Partner/Resource level. This transition requires the most long-term steady commitment, because it's the toughest transition of all to make. And second, we have to ask regularly, month after month and week after week, for the kind of face-to-face, physical contact that gets us into people's cubicles, onto their shop floors, and looking out their windows.

One good way to do this is to invite your contact in to meet your boss, and then ask for a reciprocal meeting (perhaps over lunch) to meet your contact's boss. See what kind of internal referrals you can secure through such a meeting.

Another good way to do this is to ask for a tour of the prospect's facility—plant, distribution center, headquarters, etc. During the visits, distribute business cards and collect them in return.

Yet another good way to do this is to invite your contact and his or her closest business ally (once you figure out who that is) to a public event your company sponsors, such as a seminar or a product launch.

Finally, consider improving the business side of your relationship with your contact by mailing him articles or books that are directly relevant to his or her responsibilities, and unrelated to any product or service offering of your company's. Keep track of what you send, and how your contact responds to it, in a dossier or database. These tiny investments of time and energy really will pay off with more information about the people and challenges your contact faces during the course of a working day.

Those are four good ways to get started. If you follow the advice laid out in this chapter, and keep at it over a period of four months, you will have laid the groundwork for expanding your knowledge of the challenges faced by other players in the organization besides your current contact. That's the first thing you have to do if you plan to move from Vendor to Partner/Resource.

Now let's consider the second level. At the **Supplier** level, we are not quite the status quo, yet. We have probably not been on the person's radar screen as long as the person at that third stage has, but we have had at least one or two sales, usually more than one.

At this point, we are on the short list. If they want a quote or a proposal, we are included on the list of people they reach out to for that. But that, of course, is a long way away from being on the short list of people who actually end up getting that business on a regular basis.

Sometimes after we do our first piece of business with a company, and we get a request for a quote or a request for a proposal, we may be tempted to assume that there's been a major shift in our status at that company. "Hey, look at this," we think, "A Request for Proposal (RFP). I'm in a great situation." If only it were that easy!

Inevitably, I find that the RFP is composed by some entity that begins with the letter C.

The first C entity is a committee within the organization. My tip-off here is if the document is extremely long. We must be careful here, though, because the simple fact that a committee wrote the criteria is no guarantee that the committee itself will vote to determine the provider. More likely, the committee, if it plays any role at all, will make a recommendation to an individual, the decision maker, and that recommendation may or may not carry a great deal of weight in determining the final outcome. In any event, I'm going to be wondering, "Who's on the committee?"

Another C author for the RFP that we could conceivably be looking at is the consultant. In that case, I am wondering, "Who is this consultant and how is he paid—by a fee or by a percentage of the deal that ensues?" The answer to that question is sometimes very interesting—once it comes out. The unfortunate thing is, both in terms of our questions about the committee and our questions about the consultant, there's nobody for us to ask. At least not if we're at the Supplier level. More often than not, when we get that call telling us that we're "one of the teams" invited to respond to the quote, our contact either won't, or can't, answer either of the questions I'm suggesting here: "Who's on the committee?" or "Who is this consultant?"

But you know what is even more important than who is on the committee or who the consultant is? Who decided that there would be a committee? Who decided that a consultant would get the task of establishing the criteria for the job? If you are on the committee, who put you on the committee? If you are a consultant, who engaged you as a consultant? That is even more important than the content of any document of two authors or those two sources could put together. Why did they choose to use any consultant at all, and what was the process by which that consultant was chosen?

It would be nice to know, but at this Supplier level, we rarely have any kind of access to that information. That is why I rarely put in a bid on these kinds of things when I don't have a Vendor or Partner relationship in place.

Notice that I said *rarely*, not *never*.

The last C is the C-level decision maker. If the RFP that you are looking at is short, concise, and direct, and has just a few things on it, it is very likely that it was actually composed by a single, high-ranking person within the organization. If that is the case, I may be able to make some kind of headway by connecting directly with that C-level person to discuss what is in that RFP, why it's there, and maybe even whether it can be revised further.

There is a fourth, and quite disturbing, candidate as a C author to the RFP. You will notice that I did not mention the RFP issue when we were at the vendor stage. Did you wonder why that was? The answer is that once you reach the vendor stage, *you* are dictating the terms of the RFP, or at least influencing those terms in a profound way so that they favor your company. That process of influence is more or less consolidated when you get to that third stage. That means that if we are back at the second stage—only a supplier, we really do have to take into account the possibility that we are hooking up with the fourth C as author, or at least as a major influencer, of the company's request for a proposal.

If I am at the second stage, have a reasonable level of industry experience, and do not recognize any of the terms in the RFP, *somebody else* has written it in such a way that makes it less incomprehensible to companies who might want to bid. If I can see that kind of thing happening, I should know that there's a very good chance that the competition is in fact trying to lock me out of any chance of getting that business. Well, all of that is going to affect the amount of time and effort that I put in on that particular RFP. If my competition is already there, already at that third level, and has already created the terms of the game, then I am not going to spend days or weeks trying to strategize how best to respond to that proposal, because it is a very low level of likelihood that I am actually going to get that business. In fact, there's a decent chance that my competition may be trying to lure me into the mistake of investing lots of time and energy on a proposal I can't possibly win.

Mastering Your Key Accounts

There's a very simple test I have for determining whether it makes sense to invest time, effort, and energy in responding to an RFP if I'm at this second, or Supplier, level of the relationship. If I can generate a good conversation with someone who is willing to consider revising some element of the RFP then I will work on trying to get the deal.

If, however, I can't have any kind of conversation with anyone who has any authority to alter any of the criteria, I don't submit a bid. By the same token, if I do track down someone who could change the criteria, but that person tells me that it's impossible to change a comma anywhere, and keeps telling me to follow the instructions (no matter how long, misguided, or pointless they may be), then I have a pretty good idea that this business isn't going to be my business. I don't bother putting the time in, and I don't submit a bid.

Obviously, if I'm down at the second level, I'm going to have to build up some strategies for learning more about what's going on inside this company. I may not even have a meaningful contact within the organization; I may get blizzarded with relatively shallow communications from five or six people at a time, perhaps via e-mail or over the phone.

In that case, my aim is pretty simple: Ask politely and persistently for a face-to face appointment with the person who seems to have the highest level of knowledge and authority in the organization. (Often, this turns out to be someone you might not expect to be willing to be taken out on a business lunch, but who knows just about everything worth knowing.)

Let's look now at the fourth, and lowest, level, the **Seller** level.

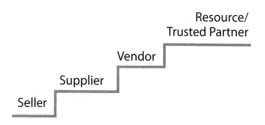

At this level, we have just made our first sale. This is obviously not a key account situation.

At least, at this stage, we actually have a sale to talk about. Note that a business relationship does not begin until we have made our first sale. That's the good news: we've made that sale, and the relationship is in fact beginning. But obviously, we have a lot of work to do in terms of identifying the world in which the person who bought from us is living.

It's a beginning, though, and that shouldn't be minimized. We now know that this company is definitely worth investing time, effort, and energy in, which is something we can't really say about a prospect. I can't tell you how many times I've talked to salespeople who invested massive amounts of time and energy with people who obviously had no inclination whatsoever to buy from them. Such salespeople say things such as: "I am really working on that relationship. I am putting all this time and effort into improving that relationship. Pretty soon I am going to find a way to get the person to agree to accept tickets to our special company luxury box so that they can watch a ball game, and that will definitely improve the relationship, and then they'll buy from us."

I have news for you. If the person has never bought anything from you and you are still plugging all these resources to improve the relationship, there is not much chance of a purchase happening. (Check the odds yourself. Total up all of the people who agree to make major purchase decisions, with their career on the line, based on somebody taking them out to a ball game.)

The relationship actually begins once we have a mutually beneficial decision to work with each other. That starts at this first level where we are a seller and a person has just bought something from us. There is only so much you can do with relationship building, in the absence of payment, that will give you a sense of whether there is any relationship fundamentally to improve. The decision to pay you for something really does change the relationship in a dramatic and profound way. It is only after that point that I can make mistakes and then prove that I either am, or am not, capable of recovering from the mistake in a way that still merits both trust and ongoing infusions of cash. Trust that only exists in some abstract sense just doesn't matter. Once you start getting paid, a person's decision to trust you plays out in an entirely different way. Before you start being paid, there really isn't any trust at all, at least not in the business sense of the word. There's just a social relationship. That's nice, but it's not something we should confuse with selling.

DYNAMICS OF THE BUSINESS RELATIONSHIP

What is going to affect our progress as we start at the low level, the seller level, and move our way up to the resource level? What are the dynamics at play in those business relationships, and what do we need to focus on over time in order the speed up our forward progress?

As it turns out, there are five dynamics of a business relationship that affect our progress from the bottom level of the four-step selling model to the top level. They are:

1. Time

2. Trust

3. Reliability

4. How much they like you

5. How much they respect you

All five of these factors affect the quality of the relationship, the information you are able to uncover, and the speed with which you move up on the scale from seller to partner/resource. Let's look first at **time**.

Contrary to popular belief, it is not how much time a salesperson spends with a customer or prospect that matters most. We can be on the seller list for years or decades, and spend hours with the contact, and still stay at the second level of that relationship model. It is really the quality of the time that we spend with the person that makes the most difference.

That principle holds true on the grand scale—as in the quality of time you spend with a customer over a period of five years will in fact determine the forward progress you experience in that relationship. But this is true on the small scale as well. Let's look at this on the microlevel, because that's the easiest way to illustrate it.

If I spend an hour talking to somebody about the weather, that hour is actually kind of like five minutes of quality time. (Unless, of course, the weather is deeply relevant to the person's business, and I tie the discussion to the person's professional and business goals.) On the other hand, if I speak to a person for an hour about something that is personally important to him or her—how to get a big raise or a promotion—all of a sudden that hour becomes more like three hours of quality time.

So my first quality issue, when I'm considering the amount of time I'm spending with my key accounts, is what we talk about with regard to selling. Are we focusing on what they do, how they do it, when they do it—both for them and the organization? In other words, am I making a conscious effort to focus on what they are doing within the department, what they are doing in terms of their own career, what the organization is doing to deal with competitive challenges, and so on?

Now, I cannot always get to that important kind of conversation in the first few discussions with the customer. Sometimes if I've had only one discussion and the person called in to buy something from me, I am going to have to find other ways, settings, and venues to try and address those more important "do-based" issues.

It is quite possible that some of the people we want to turn into key accounts are people who are buying from us on a regular basis but are not giving us any kind of meaningful information about the other opportunities that exist in the account. It is possible that we are really total strangers with that person on many levels, and that the purchase decision has played out in a pretty superficial way. In such a situation, we are quite vulnerable to competitive challenges, so we want to find a way to make the time that we spend with people much more meaningful. How do we do that?

One way to do that is to look at the number of visits and the number of separate events that we suggest. We want to find several different ways to communicate with this person, because the number of contacts really is going to affect how the person perceives the growth of the relationship.

Just think about this comparison: If we are speaking with one customer for an hour, at the end of that meeting we might leave the meeting and still be more or less total strangers. Now compare that situation with the one where I speak to somebody three times for twenty minutes each. At the end of that third twenty-minute meeting I have actually probably got a little bit better relationship going.

The frequency of my face-to-face interaction with this person actually may help me to move forward into that do-based questioning model. I'm going to consider investing my time in smaller chunks, when the opportunity arises to do so, because I want to expedite the progress in the relationship, and get the person to feel comfortable opening up to me.

Here is another aspect of the time equation that we sometimes leave out: Where are we spending the time? As in where, physically, are the meetings taking place? Where are we when we are speaking? If I speak to somebody while that person is sitting behind a desk, that it is very different than if we are meeting and walking down the hallway to their office. Think about it. If I am having a discussion with a new customer while he is in his office, he may be the king of his domain in that setting, but I may notice that he has a totally different set of social obligations when we are walking from Point A to Point B in his workplace. By changing the locale, I can actually get a little bit better sense of both what this person's day looks like and also where he actually fits within the organization. I'll also start getting a better idea of who else I might want to ask in the organization.

It is even possible that a very brief walk through the hallway or a walk across the factory floor may illustrate to me that this person really has very little knowledge whatsoever of what is going on in the company. When I watch how other employees relate to this person, I am going to learn a lot about how much respect this person has from employees, how much interaction takes place, and what kind of interaction takes place.

Now, suppose we were to meet at my office. That would change the equation as well. There would be a whole different set of social factors at work. For instance, if I introduce the person to my boss and my boss asks if my contact minds if he calls his boss, then my boss, being perceived as an authority figure, may get a positive answer to that, where I might have gotten an ambiguous or a negative answer. (Try it—it's a fascinating exercise in social role-playing.)

So where we are really does change the relationship. Knowing this, my preference is to first spend some time meeting people in their office and then change the setting somehow. Maybe they can come to my office, meet my boss, and so forth. Maybe the next meeting after that we could meet at a neutral site like a restaurant.

■ ■ ■

The second business dynamic we want to look at is **trust**.

The only way to really get people to trust you is to act in a trustworthy manner, and that is especially true when it comes to a relationship where you want access to information. Here as elsewhere, you get what you give.

I have to model the behavior of keeping my contact in the loop by letting him know what is going on. I have to say things such as, "Listen. I came across an article that I really think has competitive information in it that could affect your team's performance next year. I'll mail it to you."

Or, "We are going to be marketing to somebody else in another division of your company over on the West Coast. Here's who we're thinking of contacting. Do you have any advice for me?"

Or, "We are going to be sending out a brochure that references you as a client. Could you take a look at it for me and give me your opinion?"

If I keep my contact in the loop, I am going to earn points as being a trustworthy contact. I finally get to the point when I am saying to my contact, "Hey, can you introduce me to the CFO?" or "Can I make some suggestions about some things you might want to consider including in your RFP?" Ideally, we want to demonstrate that we're worthy of that kind of trust before we come out and demand it from the other person.

By the way, if you jump the gun and ask for an introduction to some highly placed person in the organization very early on in the relationship, and your contact turns you down, there's only one possible reason for that. You haven't yet demonstrated that you're trustworthy.

■ ■ ■

Let's look now at **reliability**. Once upon a time, reliability in the world of sales meant "If there is a problem, then call me." I don't think that's good enough anymore. I think in today's world you have got to go beyond that definition of reliability and develop a new definition of reliability that is anticipatory. You have to respond intelligently to problems before they take place.

The world is already full of discussions where people tell us, "Sorry your computer isn't working, but you should have called us when this first happened. The warranty expired three days ago." Reading from the rulebook is a great way to convince people not to turn into customers. My sense is that salespeople really don't need any more conversations like that in their client base than they already have. If your customer service department is going to end up talking to your unhappy customers like that, then you're just going to have to find a way to reach out to your customers before they feel exasperated enough to call customer service.

What customers are looking for is conversations where they can tell that the person they're dealing with really is willing to act on their behalf, to be an ambassador for them within the hallways of the organization, be pointed in the right direction *before* there's a crisis. If we want to win repeat business from someone, we'd better be willing to tell that person,

"Hey, I noticed your system's warranty is about to expire next month. Is there anything you want us to evaluate?"

Take the initiative. Raise the tough issues yourself. Offer to take on some of the burden of problem solving. Propose solutions ahead of time. The payoff will be extraordinary. Customers will look for ways to stick with you, despite competitive pressures, and despite pricing challenges. They'll realize that you—not just your company, but you in the role of your company's roving ambassador and proactive problem-solver—really do offer the best long-term value.

■ ■ ■

The next dynamic has to do with **how much they like you**. You really cannot make people like you, but you can do things that will increase the odds of their finding it easy to like you.

Very early on in a social conversation, we relax with a new acquaintance and look out for things that we may have in common with them, and the way we usually do that is we delve into each other's past. We say things like "Where did you go on vacation? Oh, I went there, it was great." "Where did you go to school? Oh, my brother-in-law went there, that's a great school." "Don't you hate it when the traffic is backed up? My commute took me an hour this morning, what was yours like?"

The moment the two people find anything or anyone in common they have greased the conversational wheels. Well, I can do more of that in my business meetings by making a conscious choice to delve into the other person's past. For instance, I am going to ask everybody I meet how long they have been at that company. By the way, one of the reasons I am asking that is that later on I am going to compare how long my contact has been there with how long my competitor has been there. Maybe if the competitor has been there ten years and my contact has only been there two years, there's somebody else I should talk to.

So I ask every new contact, "How long have you been here?" Then I ask, "What were you doing beforehand?" I focus in a relaxed way on the person's background and history, just as though I were in a social situation (which I am), and the answers I get back tell me a lot. If when I ask you what were you doing before and you tell me you were the assistant to this position and then you got a promotion recently, that tells me something important. You probably do not know any more today than you knew earlier before you got that promotion. If you tell me that you have been with this company for twenty-two years and you have never been anywhere else, and you know everything there is to know about the place, that's a very different set of assumptions. On the other hand, you could say to me, "I was running the same kind of operation for the Big Corporation of America, and this company recruited me in about six months ago." Those are three very different situations. But notice that, as I am uncovering information, I am also uncovering things that this person may have in common with me, and then I emphasize those things whenever possible.

Another question I ask is, "How did you get from there to here? How did you get from that beginning point in your career to this spot you are occupying right now?" These pretty easy questions are usually associated with the meeting and greeting phase, and I like to be able to ask them to uncover business information and identify commonalities. If I know a person this contact used to work with, if I find any parallel with the person's education or work background, or if we held a similar position at some point, it's going to be easier for that person to decide to like me.

■ ■ ■

The last dynamic is **respect**. Ideally, what you want to do is get people to respect you for being nice and knowledgeable, but the problem in business is that if you are too smart, smarter even than the customer, people might not actually respect you for that; you might be intimidating to that person. On the other hand, if you are not quite as smart as the other person, you may be perceived as useless. Basically, if you stop to think about it, you've got a choice between being seen as useless and being seen as intimidating!

I'm exaggerating, of course. You can strike a balance. The best way to win respect from your customers is to know what you do not know and identify your own strengths and areas of expertise. In fact, have something to add in terms of value that you are going to provide for his or her organization. You really are an expert at how to diagnose a problem that is connected to your product or service and how to implement that product or service. What you don't know—and shouldn't claim to know—is everything that makes this person's situation unique. That's what you want to ask questions about. If you're up front about your knowledge gaps on that score, you will win respect from the other person.

Let me tell you something about being a sales trainer, because we have a challenge that has to do with respect—and I think it is probably something similar to the challenges that you face as a salesperson. It is very tempting for the people in my training groups to think, "Oh, what does he know; he does not work in our particular business."

Even if you tell them, "I actually did work in your business once," they will say, "Well, that does not make any difference; you are a trainer now, and a lot of things have happened since you worked in the business." They're basically looking for a reason not to respect your insights. "You're a trainer in a company and you don't really know what we're up against."

I think that even if I were currently selling in their industry, I have a feeling I would still hear, "Well, it is different here at this company. It is a totally different situation, different location, different market, and so on." Yet somehow we've trained over 750,000 people. The CEO of the company really did decide that he wanted me to train these people who are saying, "We're different; you don't really understand our world."

My point is, we are experts. We just have to use our questioning skills to help them distinguish what we know from what we do not know. We have to be forthright about the information we need in order to make an analysis of the situation. We can't get distracted from that. If we're not experts, and we're not asking questions experts would ask, then we have no business asking for a meeting with the person in the first place.

In your world—not the world of training, but the world of selling your product—I'm thinking you run into the same phenomenon we do.

What do they think you know about their business? Nothing, unless they hear you ask lots of do-based questions about how they do what they do that demonstrates to them that you know something about your side of the field.

The key to winning respect is asking questions that subtly demonstrate your own past experience, yet still focus on what the other person is doing. Ask questions about what they do and frame those questions in the right way. Watch what happens. If we try to give any kind of help before we ask intelligent questions, the respect evaporates.

Ask, listen, and learn, *then* help. Otherwise what you say is not going to win respect, and it is not going to be perceived as helpful. It will be more like unsolicited advice, more like a Band-Aid and not a long-term solution. It will sound like something that is generic, not customized, something that won't fit. But if we ask and listen and learn and then help, then they will know you know how they are different. Then you can tailor and make valuable your product, because you will have won some respect by fitting and shaping it to their world in their language.

If you do that—if you ask, listen, learn and then help—they will respect you enough to let you lead the sales process, and they really will let you help them.

WHAT WE'RE UP AGAINST

59

We've talked about the importance of improving communication, and we've seen the five dynamics where that improvement can play out. Now, let's look at what is going to be standing in the way.

Suppose that the very next thing that needs to happen for me to close the sale is that the contact's boss has to get into the conversation. (That is certainly a very common outcome in terms of key account selling.) I have to ask myself, when will that happen? If the answer to that is *I don't know*, then guess what, the answer means that we have not really strategized the very next thing needed to move the sale forward.

If my contact has not agreed to that, then I cannot count that person as a prospect. If I do not contact the person's boss, what are the odds of eventually getting past the interview phase and into the presentation and the closing stages? Slim. Not impossible, but reduced.

I want to maximize my time with people who are likely to buy. As I go from step to step to step, I am beginning to realize that as I am strategizing, the whole sales process is really all about communication. I haven't yet communicated why it makes sense for both of us for the person's boss to get involved in the conversation. I need to make some kind of effort to connect more meaningfully on this point before I invest more time and energy in this project.

There are several things that may be preventing me from doing that, and I should understand exactly what they are. Let's imagine that two people are having a conversation; one is a customer, and the other is a salesperson.

The salesperson is thinking about what he is going to say, but there are a lot of things that will affect and distort that message before it reaches the customer: the salesperson's vocabulary, choice of body position, or his or her ability to establish appropriate eye contact, for example. All of these elements can prevent us from communicating clearly what we thought the customers were communicating. Just to make matters worse, 65 percent of all communication is nonverbal body language, but we as salespeople tend to focus on memorizing words to say, and we often ignore or overlook important parts of the body language message.

Consider, then, all of the physical and psychological barriers that prevent another person from hearing everything I am saying. It is as if I were talking to my contact as I notice my tie slung over my shoulder, and everything I say from that point on would be a huge waste of time because all I could focus on is my strangely misplaced tie.

Communication barriers can be anything. The clients could be listening for some important phone call. Maybe he did not understand some of the terminology I've used. Or it could be, I said something that sounded like "milk," and he thought, "Oh, that reminds me, I have to pick up milk on my way home." Or, the person's attention span goes in and out.

People are basically listening in and out of our message the entire time. And then, just to make matters worse, when they *think* about what they thought I said, they lose even more of the message. Even if this customer is the absolute final decision maker, more often than not in the key account sales he will in fact talk to others about the discussion that we just had. People that I may never meet.

That's a whole new challenge. Let's look at it a little more closely now.

Let's call the other person our customer is talking to after I leave Customer Two, or C2.

Customer One, or C1, may be the decision maker, but C2 is, at the very least, an Influencer. That person may be above or below the level that my contact is on, but he can definitely influence the sale. The boss will run an idea past the secretary. The head person will run the idea past the chairman of the board, the middle-level person will communicate up and down.

By the time C1 tells C2 what he thought I said, maybe an hour, month, or week has passed. The point is that some amount of time has passed, and all of a sudden, the discussions of my products and services not only have to deal with all the same obstacles I had to face (body language, terminology, eye contact, etc.) but the passage of time and the fallibility of the human memory have conspired to make the discussion between C1 and C2 sound something like this:

> *C1:* I meant to tell you something.
>
> *C2:* Oh yeah? What's up?
>
> *C1:* I met with a salesperson from the, oh, what is the name of that company? I forgot. Anyway, he's working on something for us. I'm supposed to talk to him next week.

Now maybe I am exaggerating, but not by much.

How much of my intended message actually reached C2? Close to nothing.

But what did I think happened?

Well, usually, we salespeople think that a lot more got accomplished than actually did. Do you remember the old *Star Trek* TV series, when Spock could do a Vulcan mind meld, instantly downloading the contents of somebody else's head into his head? Well, in sales, we think that is what we are doing when we have a sales meeting, only we think that we can download the contents of our head into somebody else, and that they'll do the same. We want to pretend the person has a perfect memory and is willing to use it on our behalf with everyone else in the company, and we want to talk ourselves into believing that those barriers to communication don't exist. But they do.

We talked to C1, and he looked at us intently and nodded his head as though it were all very interesting.

However, here's what C1 *really* hears:

"Let me tell you about us. We blah blah blah blah blah blah blah."

And then C1 says, "Got it! I'll tell the others!"
Like he could!

■ ■ ■

Here's the moral: people barely communicate. If you take that initial assumption, you begin to understand that your job is not only to send the right message, but to help the other person reinforce it intelligently over time.

Basically, you have two possible guiding strategies for doing this, both of which can lead to improved communication between you and your contact, and, ultimately, greater exposure to the other people in the organization. These strategies work hand-in-hand, and their aim is to provide you with the opportunity to repeat, reframe, and reinforce your message many times with many people.

Guiding Strategy #1: "I just had a brilliant idea." You come up with some incredible new way to help your contact do what he or she does better, and you incorporate within that idea a blank spot that requires information your contact simply can't provide. (The company's strategic focus in addressing technological change, for instance.) In order to complete the picture, and develop the recommendation that matches the situation perfectly, you suggest a round-table meeting/presentation/bull session with all the key people.

Guiding Strategy #2: "I'm not that kind of salesperson." If the contact insists that you jump through all the hoops, do all the work, and invest significant resources, and, at the same time, refuses you any access to any of the key people in the account, draw the line. Say, "I don't work that way. I'm going to need your help tracking down the right people if I'm going to do this job right for you." (Obviously, you'll have to fine-tune the message so it matches your contact and his situation, but you get the idea.) If this approach doesn't get you anywhere, reach out to someone else in the organization on your own.

60

IT WORKED! NOW WHAT?

It paid off! You connected with your contact well enough to get him to agree to help you connect with some of the Influencers and decision makers who operate elsewhere in the organization. Now what do you do?

There are eight things you have to do to prepare for a meeting with a new contact within your key account. The first four are generic, and apply to every single such meeting you will go on.

Pre-meeting Planning Item #1: Practice answering the question, "What do we sell?" You must be able to concisely describe the products and services your organization offers and how, specifically, those products and services benefit your customers. You must have so much practice doing this that the answer is purposeful, automatic, and extremely confident. If you answer the question in totally different ways every single time it comes up, you need to practice.

Just for safety's sake, take two minutes right now and write down your best response to the question "What do we sell?" Write at least four sentences.

Pre-meeting Planning Item #2: Practice answering the question, "What makes us different from the competition?" Remember that they are using something already in the status quo. Think about it. A prospect may well have one and only one way of distinguishing potential vendors (for example, price). You should be familiar with all the differences between you and the organizations you're competing against, and be ready to discuss them. You will need to prepare many answers to this question to suit many different situations, so it is wise to come up with a number of examples.

Here again, you should take two minutes and write down as many factors as you can that could distinguish you from a competitor.

Pre-meeting Planning Item #3: Practice answering the question, "What makes us better than the competition?" No, this is not the same as the question above. Be prepared to explain, briefly and enthusiastically, why someone did in fact decide to buy from you, rather than from someone else. If you're not comfortable doing this, you're in the wrong line of work! Take the initiative. Do the research. Find out why your company's number one client decided to buy from you, rather than anyone else. Repeat the process until you have between six and ten relevant success stories.

Yes, this will take a while, but please do not continue to the next item until you have identified the success stories, and committed them to paper.

Pre-meeting Planning Item #4: Be prepared to complete the sentence, "Even though we're not always the least expensive option, people buy from us because . . ." If you don't know, find out!

Write down at least one draft of your answer to this question before proceeding.

The written component of this chapter—actually writing down the responses to each of these pre-meeting planning items—is extremely important, Please don't skip it! Once you do this exercise, you'll be better prepared for each and every meeting or discussion with a key account that you take part in.

There are four more steps you must take before meeting with any new contact within one of your key accounts. Unlike the first four, each of these is going to require a very close focus on the particular company you'll be interacting with.

Pre-meeting Planning Item #5: Do the right research. There are three kinds of things that I put under the umbrella of research. The first is conventional research. You have to say to yourself, "Are my competitors, who are also trying to win a chunk of my business at this account, doing any research on this? If so, what are they likely to be doing?" I have to do at least the level of research they would do. At a minimum, that probably means going to the Web site, or looking at the annual report. I should definitely talk to colleagues who have knowledge that I don't about what's happening at this particular account. Why? I know my competitors will be checking the Web site, looking at the annual report, and talking to all of their people about the company's history. If you're dealing with a large company, you have to assume that your competition is covering more ground than it would with a really small company. You can't walk into IBM and say, "So, you're IBM. Tell me what you guys do."

The second type of research is on your own company's record of similar success stories with other accounts that match well with this particular account. My guess is that you could be taking advantage of this more than you are now. Even really experienced salespeople very rarely have a complete understanding of the whole range of customers that fall into parallel categories with the key account that they are responsible for. You have to be willing to go to your sales manager, or maybe even somebody higher up in the company, and sit down with them for fifteen to twenty minutes and ask them, "What have we done with software companies before? What have we done with oil companies? What have we done with companies that do work for the government? What have we done with healthcare companies?" Whatever category your specific key account falls into (and there may be more than one), you have to do some internal detective work and take advantage of company stories, facts, figures, and anecdotes that connect to similar situations within your account. You want to be able to walk in and say, "By the way, did you know we've worked with the following companies in your type of business?" If we have actual results for each of those companies that we can cite case studies for, we are going to be better off during our discussions with our contact at the key account. (By the way, doing this kind of research gives you confidence and a sense of purpose that can make a huge difference in your discussions.)

Finally, research the contact networks that exist within the business, at least to the best of your ability. This is probably the hardest form of research, but you can start by brainstorming with colleagues about what you already know about the way this organization is set up, as well as how likely it is to match up internally with other companies you've worked with. For example, let's say you are about to have a sales meeting at a bank that you want to acquire more business from. A good question to ask in preparation for that meeting would be, "What is the likely structure within this bank, compared to all the other banks I've worked with?" Chances are they have a retail banking unit and they have business-to-business banking. They have somebody who is the head of retail banking and who controls all the banking products and services they sell through branches. On the other hand, they also have a head of mortgage banking, who is responsible for specific products in that area. The people who are selling mortgages have to report to the head of mortgages, but they also have a direct line of responsibility to the people who run the bank branches. Let's assume we are taking a look at this from the point of view of my company, which offers sales training. We want to think about all the different possible decision makers and influencers, as well as the likely challenges that we might face. It is not that you are necessarily right about all this contact network research and brainstorming, but doing this does allow you to walk in the door with an assumption. And that gives you something you can be "righted" about, a point of entry into the discussion.

Pre-meeting Planning Item #6: Brainstorm your questions. I want to prepare, in advance, all of the questions that I might possibly have. I am putting myself in this contact's shoes, and I am thinking to myself, "I wonder if the bank really does have trouble capturing new business because it is perceived as being inferior than the larger banks? I wonder what the bank's ratio is of new business to existing business? I wonder if the bank is even trying to go after new business?" And all of these sorts of questions are going to lead to different questions that I want to pose during this meeting with my contact. And of course, the more background I have with this person, the better off that questioning is going to go. You will find more detailed information on the types of questions to ask in Chapters 63, 64, and 65.

Pre-meeting Planning Item #7: Create the flow. How am I going to create the flow that is going to get me into the conversation? Specifically, that means, how am I going to open the meeting? How am I going to engage that person in a good conversation? What things can I say that will open up the conversation in a way that is more likely to lead to a Next Step? Specifically, how am I going to strategize the very opening of the meeting? What happens after the pleasantries? Is my contact going to be a part of the meeting? Am I going to ask him to debrief the new person on what has happened up to this point? Or am I going to do that? If so, does my contact know what I'm going to say? What is my very first question going to be, and how am I going to transition into it?

These are the things that go into creating the flow of the meeting. Now, a lot of salespeople skip this step. But you know, when you think about it, there's a great reason not to skip this step. If you have a good conversation with this new person within the account—and by "good conversation," I mean something that could go anywhere from twenty to forty-five minutes and results in you returning to work on some new possibility of business—then you might get paid.

On the other hand, if the conversation does not go well, you probably will not get paid.

The whole thing *hinges* on having a good conversation. Would you agree with methat planning the flow is worth it? I thought so.

It is worth trying to determine ahead of time exactly how you are going to transition into a specific topic, and particularly how you are going to open the meeting. You will find that if you feel really comfortable when opening the meeting, then as a general rule, the meeting will go well. If you feel uncomfortable and stiff, and come off a little awkward and a little tentative at the beginning of the meeting, then even if you have a great internal referral to this person, the chances are the meeting will not go well. So it really does not make any sense at all to just hope that everything works out well at the beginning of the meeting. We want to make sure it starts off well. We want to open up with a sequence that is going to get you exactly where you want to go, which means you have to strategize it. I'll give you some more information on how to do this in Chapter 61, which covers what I call the PIPA sales interview model.

Pre-meeting Planning Item #8: Decide on your primary and backup Next Steps. The eighth and last thing I want to do before I meet with this person is think about how I am going to get back. Like a good pool player who sets up each shot with the last shot, I want to review all the angles and say to myself, "How is what I am about to do at the beginning of the meeting going to point me toward what I want to have happen at the end of the meeting? Specifically, what do I want to have happen at the end of the meeting? What does my primary Next Step look like, and what does my secondary Next Step look like? In other words, what kind of Next Step am I going to ask for if I don't get the one I'm after?"

Think of it this way. When you put your hand on that door, sixty minutes from that moment, the odds are that you are probably going to either already have walked out or be walking out, and you are either going to be walking out with a Next Step, or without that kind of Next Step. So think about what you want from this situation in terms of Next Steps that move the sale forward.

Once you know where you want the meeting to end, you are more likely to successfully structure it to get there. You are not trying to have a great meeting for the purposes of having stimulating conversation. You want to get to a certain point. That is the whole reason you want to have a good discussion, and of course, if you have created both a Plan A and a Plan B, there is a much greater likelihood of that happening.

You'll find Appendix B a detailed discussion of Next Steps you can ask for.

61 THE PERFECT MEETING

Imagine if every time you left a meeting with somebody who represented repeat business with your company, you got out to the parking lot and you saw a scorer's table. There, sitting at the table, are Olympic scorers holding up signs with number scores like in the Olympics: 6, 2, 8, perfect 10. Imagine the pressure!

Well, suppose those judges were operating secretly, without making your life more stressful. Suppose that each meeting really did culminate in a score. If you analyzed all those scores and kept track of them over the course of a year, you would realize that sometimes you posted low scores and sometimes you posted high scores. Here's my point: if you just looked at the things you do in your very best meetings, this is what you would see.

P
I
P
A

You may not realize it, but you really are doing something right. What I want to show you are the elements of PIPA. These elements aren't "new" ways to sell to your key accounts, but things you are *already* doing right in your best meetings with your contacts. I want to help you become more consistent in the ways that you conduct those meetings, so you can consistently create such meetings to a high standard and maybe have another one or two good meetings a week.

Let's start by looking at the end of the process and then reverse it to see how you arrived at that point. When you walk into a meeting you are going to say hello, and then somehow over a half hour or forty-five minutes, you have to get from hello to . . . what? Well, obviously, you have to get that end goal of having a Next Step.

You're looking for a clear commitment to a meeting with you at some future point, something that will occupy a position on the calendar of your contact at this key account. So, the A of the PIPA formula stands for "AGREE to a Next Step."

P

I

P

Agree

The customer needs to agree to the Next Step, whatever that is. It could be to start rolling out your program. It could be to meet again. It could be any number of things, but it still occupies that position on the person's calendar. Meetings should invariably end with some kind of a clear Next Step. The question is how do we get there? Somehow we have to get from hello to that.

Well, before I can get you to agree to a Next Step I have to suggest some kind of a Next Step. I could say something such as, "Hey, why don't we get together again next Tuesday at 3:00 P.M.?" The thing is, though, for me to get the person to agree to a Next Step, I have got to position that Next Step as being:

- Potentially easy to agree to

- Potentially helpful to a person who is thinking about possibly buying

I have to describe how that Next Step could help that person, and the best way to do that is waht is called called **Parable Selling**.

P
I
Parable Selling/Present Next Step
Agree

I am going to paint a picture of how the prospect and I could work together, and I am going to do that in a certain way. Here's what it might sound like:

> "I worked with another client who was a lot like you. He also had a similar challenge with keeping track of payroll, and what we did for his company was very helpful. I brought in my technical person and he was able to spend an hour learning about the client's system and processes and clarifying how we might be able to work together. He helped everybody to get a fix on the specifics of the project. Maybe that is a way for you and me to continue. Maybe we should do that together? How about if I bring Roscoe, my technical support person, in next Tuesday at 3:00 P.M.?"

Notice how I used the story of how I helped somebody else as a way for the client to visualize what I could do for him. That builds reassurance and, not coincidentally, it can also be used as a strategy for helping me to gain access within the account.

Now I have a question for you. When did I think of that Next Step that I wanted to ask about to close that meeting? Did I think about it just on the spur of the moment or two minutes before I walked out the door?

No! I knew that Next Step before I walked in. What I was trying to figure out was which story I could tell during the meeting that would point me toward the Next Step I wanted!

The parable I told was a justification for asking for that Next Step. What I came up with was a relevant success story that showed how I had done a similar thing with another account that reminded me of this one. That is how I positioned the Next Step, and I am going to ask you to figure that out as well in your meetings with your contacts at key accounts. I want you to start taking what you learn in the meeting and make the Next Step the logical outcome,of that discussion. You have to find ways to tie that Next Step to the specific discussion that you are having. That brings us to interviewing and information, the I of the PIPA formula.

P
Interview/Information
Parable Selling/Present Next Step
Agree

What am I going to learn in the **Interview/Information** phase that can enable me to connect to the Next Step that I really knew I was thinking about before I walked in the door? This second component of the PIPA list is where I am going to ask all those do-based questions; what they do, how they do it, where they do it, etc. Not only am I going to ask about what the company does as an organization, but I am also going to ask about what this person's individual goals are; what his career goals are; what his goals are for the department; what he'd like to see himself being responsible for six months, a year, eighteen months, two years from now. I'm also going to ask where he came from and what he was doing a year ago. I am looking for information both on the organizational level and on the personal level.

P

Interview/Information
(Organizational level/Personal level)
Parable Selling/Present Next Step
Agree

What I want to have at the end of the meeting is a Next Step postitoned that we can both agree on. The key to that is to pull that Next Step out of the information that I am gatherering. Well, how do I get this person, who twenty minutes ago may have been totally preoccupied and may have been focused on something completely different, to tell me all about himself and his company? How do I pull that off?

The answer is here, in that first P.

Present

Interview/Information
(Organizational level/Personal level)
Parable Selling/Present Next Step
Agree

The first P in PIPA stands for *present*, but it is not the kind of presenting where the person just talks for half an hour about the features of the product. That's basically reading the person your brochure. In this case I am talking about presenting a much shorter element called a commercial. This presentation is something you have to prepare specifically for this particular key account meeting. I'll show you how to put it together in the next chapter.

OPENING THE MEETING

In this important chapter, you'll learn how to open a meeting with a new contact in your key account. To do this (whether or not your primary contact is present), you're going to use a specially crafted commercial. This commercial has six elements to it.

- The first and most important element is that the commercial is unique to this situation. What you say has to be sculpted to meet the requirements of this single contact. In other words, if you end up meeting with this person five times, you want to build a commercial that helps you to open the meeting but does not replay information that this individual has already heard before.

- Second, the commercial has to be brief—usually between thirty and ninety seconds long.

- Third, it has to be descriptive. It has to give the person a sense of what you have been working on—and how the products and services your company offers actually relate to what this person is doing now and what its new initiatives are.

- Fourth, it has to be relevant to this person's world.

- Fifth, it has to build credibility by passing along information about your company and also about you as a person. It should tell the other person something important about your company's mission and about your role. It should be something that builds confidence in both you and your organization.

- Sixth, it should sound conversational. When I say sound conversational, I mean that it should be perceived as natural and spontaneous and off the cuff, as you deliver it. This sometimes takes a little work, because it is imperative that your commercial actually be memorized.

Sometimes when I present both of those final requirements at the same time—spontaneous and memorized—I will get some resistance from salespeople. They will say, "There is no way for me to deliver this memorized commercial and have it sound conversational. You can either have one or the other, Steve, you cannot have it be both spontaneous, memorized, *and* scripted."

Whenever I get that kind of resistance, I ask the participants to think about the last movie they saw. Did the action or did the dialogue appear scripted? Did it sound stilted? Did it sound forced or somehow canned? The vast majority of people will say, "No, it didn't sound canned, it sounded totally natural and totally spontaneous."

Then I will say, "But that's very odd, isn't it? Because, you know, for them to make a movie they have to write the script ahead of time. In order to get that scene filmed, the actor spent lot of time memorizing the lines and getting it just right."

Of course, the answer to the seeming paradox is that we have to put as much effort into preparing for this unique meeting as the actor puts into preparing for a scene. It is in practicing and internalizing the script that we are going to use that it really becomes natural, normal, and spontaneous. That is the ideal—the spontaneous feeling combined with the strange power that comes with having no doubt whatsoever about what we are going to say next. Actually, memorizing the speech and practicing it really does give you the confidence necessary to deliver it with spontaneity, and that very confidence plays out for the rest of the meeting.

The goal of the commercial is, ultimately, to create a good first impression. If you don't do that, the interviewing piece simply isn't going to work. If you build the credibility at the beginning, if you create a good first impression, and if you sound like a person worth talking to, people will be more likely answer your questions. The opposite is true, too. There are some salespeople who have consistent trouble getting meaningful responses to their questions because they never really built up the credibility that gave them the right to ask those questions in the first place. They didn't establish themselves as credible people who are worth talking to.

Sometimes people will tell me, "Steve, you can't judge a book by its cover." I hear that saying a lot in reference to first impressions and the beginnings of meetings. Sometimes people get very fond of that proverb while I am challenging them to begin the meeting with a very brief memorized commercial that helps to earn credibility and start the meeting off right. Well, if that is your feeling about now—that you can't judge a book by its cover, so why bother building a commercial—I want you to rethink that for a second. The truth of the matter is that people really do judge a book by its cover, every single solitary day. In fact, whether it's right or wrong to do so, it's pretty much a standard practice in the world of business.

Actually, from the point of view of buying and selling, there is no other way to judge a book. What are you supposed to do? Read the whole book and then decide to buy it? When was the last time *you* bought a book after reading it from beginning to end?

Whether we like it or not, people make decisions about us early in the sales meeting. They're evaluating us. They're asking questions. "Is this person worth talking to at all today? Is this meeting really worth an hour of my time? Is it worth half an hour? Is it worth one minute?"

That decision-making process unfolds the same way whether we have met with a person before or whether this is the very first meeting. People evaluate: "How much time should I give this?" In other words, we remake our first impression every time we step in the door. The very first impression, obviously, has a great deal to do with the direction of the relationship, but the thing we have to remember is that a new first impression is made with every subsequent meeting. Think of the incredibly hectic days that people have, the multiple responsibilities they have, and the many things that they have on their to-do list. We've got to establish—or reestablish—that we really do have a right to time in this person's busy schedule.

Of course, every time you make a new acquaintance with somebody in collaboration with your primary contact in the key account, you are making another brand-new first impression. That means you are going to want to start that meeting off in a way that earns some credibility and sets you up with some stature. You have to establish a commercial you can use to open the meeting. You will have to strategize that commercial based on who you are actually going to be talking to and what you are going to be talking about. You have to start the meeting out in a way that is confident, poised, and clearly directed toward a certain specific goal. If you do that, the meeting goes well. If you don't, it doesn't.

So, then, how did you get there? How did you get to the commercial? You did not simply walk in the door and deliver it. That would be a little strange, if the prospect opened the door and then instantly you launched into this thirty- or sixty-second memorized speech. No, you have to find some way to transition into that commercial. You will do that by asking a question, a very simple question.

The question has multiple variations, but it serves the single purpose of initiating the business portion of the conversation. It sounds something like this:

(*After the conclusion of small talk*) "Would it help if I went first?"

Or

(*At the conclusion of the small talk*) "Would it help if I gave you an overview of what we have done so far?"

Or

(*After the initial small talk*) "Would it help if I briefly recapped what I thought we accomplished at our last meeting?"

By asking the question after the small-talk portion of the meeting, the meet and greet, the pleasantries phase, what I am really saying to the person, in so many words, is this: "I have got something I can use to start off this meeting. How do you feel about me talking it out and putting it on the table so you can take a look at it?"

Ninety-nine percent of the time, the answer to this kind of question is yes. In those rare cases where it is not okay that I proceed along those lines, I am automatically going to be engaged in the business portion of the meeting anyway. At that point, I can move right into the interviewing phase by saying, "Okay, what direction do you think we ought to go in?" Or: "Okay, what did you want to cover today?"

Normally, the other person will be very happy to let me start the real part of the meeting.

Once I receive that assent signal, I will instantly go into my brief thirty-second to sixty-second commercial. Let me emphasize once again that I will *not* go into a twenty-minute presentation of everything I could possibly do, but only a very short commercial to launch my first question of the meeting.

In my precall planning, I established what my first question of the meeting was going to be. Again, that is what I am going to use this commercial to do: transition into that first question that I know is going to drive the meeting in the direction I want it to go. The prospect wants you to set up an agenda and say, "Here is what I have in mind, here is how I want to run the meeting." It is a very powerful signal to send at the beginning of the meeting that *you* are the person who has come up with a plan as to how it should all proceed

You really want to make sure that you are positioning yourself that way, as the person who has come for a meeting to discuss some specific ideas about how you and the prospect might be able to work more profitably together. That is part of your job description as a salesperson, to know what those ideas are so you can drive the meeting toward them. People expect that.

Here's what it sounds like in my world.

Me and Key Account Person I've Never Met Before: (We engage in a little pleasant talk, preferably something that builds commonality between us. Then a little pause, which I recognize, and fill by saying . . .)

Me: Would it help if I went first?

Key Account Person: Sure.

Me: (Here comes the commercial.) Well, DEI management group is a sales training company. We have been around twenty-seven years. We have trained 9,000 companies and we have worked with more than half a million salespeople all around the world. We work with companies like the ABC Company and the XYZ Company [and I will name companies here that are relevant to the specific situation]. I've written several books, including an international best-seller on appointment making. I have done more than X hundred programs for people in your industry. Actually, though, I have to be honest, the reason I came here today was to find out about your corner of the company. [Here comes my first question:] Can I ask you what you're doing right now to train the salespeople in this division?

Notice that it starts with the transition out of small talk, concisely hits all six of my objectives, and ends with a very specific question, one that I have chosen ahead of time. This commercial gets me very smoothly into the interview or information-gathering phase.

Out of everything I said in that commercial, what facts would the customer actually remember the next morning? Hardly any. He would have remembered the names of some companies we have dealt with—companies that were probably impressive because I would have chosen them to be so—but, he might not actually even remember the names of the companies. In fact, I know going in that most of what I say during the commercial will not stick, but I paint it with such a broad brushstroke that the contact isn't going to worry about not remembering the essentials. He might remember about people doing a lot of training, and that the company has been around a long time and has worked with a couple of interesting companies. That's it.

You know what? That is really all I want the person to hear. I really do not plan on them analyzing or evaluating anything else. Why? Because remember, this person is making up his mind about how much attention to pay to me. This person is listening but he has a heavy-duty filter over his ear. He's basically trying to figure out if this is really worth paying attention to.

If you make a habit of using this model to open your meeting, what you are going to find is that the basic structure that you use to open the meeting is inevitably going to be the same, and that's good. You want it to be the same. You want the sequence of events that lead to your first question to be something you feel absolutely, totally confident about. You don't want there to be any surprises; it is very important in this setting that you have something that you can rely on and be familiar with. Let's face it, it can be a very stressful situation to walk into somebody's office, and in that situation you really want to make sure you feel confident and comfortable about what you are saying. Well, the best way to make sure of that is simply to practice the opening and to use a certain predictable structure for getting to that first question.

You should expect to be distracted in these environments. Sometimes your primary contact will be there, introducing you to everyone you need to meet, and the person you came to see will be pleasant and gracious and warm and say, "Sit down, let's get you settled." They'll give you a cup of coffee. The whole experience will be very welcoming. Other times, you will be totally on your own, you'll walk in, introduce yourself, get next to nothing in response, and then hear the person say, "Okay, what have you got?"

You have to find a way to respond productively in both situations, and that means practicing your opening and becoming familiar with the basic structure of your transition into the interviewing phase. Under pressure, you will automatically fall back on what you are familiar with. That's why salespeople deliver those half-hour monologues about their products and services. They feel stressed out and they go back to the only thing they know well, the features of the product or the service. You have to know the opening of your meeting at least that well!

Make a commitment to practice this sequence that I have suggested. Use it as a tool that will, if you memorize it, help you put all the strange things that may have happened that day aside and focus on getting the meeting going in a productive way. You don't want to be making up your half of the meeting. You want the opening of the meeting to always go basically the same way (although you can change the lyrics to match the situation if you practice them). Make absolutely sure you are comfortable and familiar with what you are presenting. The interviews really will go better if you do that because you will not be so distracted, and you will be able to pay attention to the other person. Practice what you are going to say to open the meeting, and I guarantee you that you will be in a much better position to tune in to what the prospects say to you during the meeting.

THE ELEPHANT

So this salesperson walks into the office of a brand-new prospect at one of his key accounts, and he notices something strange. He sees that there's a large elephant standing there in the middle of the room. He stares at the elephant, looks at his prospect, then takes a seat, pulls out his brochure, and pretends there's no elephant.

It sounds like a joke. But it's serious. In fact, it's the most common obstacle to effective key accounts selling today.

While there are many questions that salespeople have been taught to ask, there are few that relate to the elephant. Most people never see or hear the elephant. Most people train themselves to ignore the elephant. This is the famous expression *the elephant in the room* that you've probably heard of.

Let me explain what I mean. The typical salesperson has his own short set of prepared questions with which to begin the discussion with someone at one of his key accounts. That salesperson is convinced that those five or six memorized questions are the best questions to ask at each and every meeting, whether they are open-ended or closed-ended. A quick look at the average results of asking those questions suggests that a different approach to interviewing might be more effective.

What is the most important thing that a salesperson really knows when he walks in the door to see someone for the first time? The person's name? Maybe. The person's title? Maybe. The company's product or service? Maybe.

But there's something else. Something much more important.

The one thing that we can count on—the one critical fact we know for sure—is that this part of the key account universe is not yet ours. That's really the only meaningful thing we know. Somebody else at this company is working with us, but this person isn't. That's the elephant in the room. So why don't we ask about that at the beginning of the meeting?

Remember: the number one competitor, for the majority of salespeople, is **status quo**. In other words, the real competition is what the prospect is doing now by force of habit. That's what matters. They do not need us, no matter how many need-based questions we may choose to ask. Frankly, if we went out of business tonight, there would be few people who would even care. (You and I would, of course, but I'm talking about the prospects we imagine have this "need" for what we offer.)

If we know that the true competitor, status quo, is standing there like an elephant in the middle of the room, why not ask about that?

Below, you will find a list of questions that you should try to work your way up to in the interview. (We'll look at the preliminaries, what has to happen *before* you get to these questions, later, but for right now I want you to look at the direction you should be pointing the discussion in.

- ☐ "I talked with (Other Contact at This Organization Who Is Working with Us), and found you are not working with us. I'm just curious, who are you using now?"

- ☐ "What did (Other Contact at This Organization Who Is Working with Us) tell you about what he and I have done so far?"

- ☐ "Is there a reason that you've chosen to use (Company X)?"

- ☐ "Can you tell me how you use the product/service you've got in place now? (Or: How does the end user work with the product/service?)"

■ "When was the last time you reviewed the product/service?" (Assuming that you don't know of any immediate problem with it. If you do know of such a problem, ask about that.)

■ "I think that we're better than (Company X), but I can't prove it if I don't know how you made the decision to go with them. How did you decide to go with them?"

Instead of ignoring the elephant, build these simple questions into the big questions you develop for your next meeting with a new contact within your key account. See if you don't uncover some important information.

KEY ACCOUNT INTERVIEWING IN DEPTH

You just read about the critical principle that I call Asking About the Elephant. In this chapter, I'm going to look in much more depth at the progression of the interviewing and information-gathering phase, in order to give you an idea of how you get to the point where you can expect to get a meaningful answer to that question.

I have to be honest. This is something you can (and should) spend a professional lifetime learning, so obviously it's going to receive more than a single chapter's worth of attention. To really address this topic, you will want to work closely with your manager or a professional sales coach. At this point, though, I want to cover this subject as fully as I possibly can within the medium of the printed page. So let's get to work.

■ ■ ■

One of the ways that I start this subject during our training programs is to acknowledge that people usually assume they have very little to learn on the subject of interviewing prospects and customers. (I often train people who have been selling for many years.) I'll start out by saying, "I'll bet nobody in this class thinks that he is not doing a good job already of asking questions within his major accounts. Am I right?" There will be a few smiles and a couple of knowing glances between participants, and a couple of people will nod their heads sagely.

It is quite rare that I get any resistance on that point; most people will agree, do in fact they believe they are already doing a good, or even a great job of asking the key account questions. And indeed, for the most part, the people I am teaching that course to have already covered the basics of interviewing. Chances are, they have been selling for a while. So one of the ways that I build some credibility with them is by showing them how much more information they *could* be getting during their meetings.

I often ask people some questions about their own current accounts, and as I do that, I will offer information from our own experience of working with key accounts. My favorite example comes from the world of banking. People who work at banks are sometimes very high-level professionals, and a lot of the people we train are likely to have been working at a bank for a very long time, about twenty or thirty years. The banker I'm training, who is now a senior vice president, probably started out as a branch manager twenty years ago. Usually, that person can think very easily of a customer he brought on board twenty years ago. This person might have been someone he personally brought to the bank.

The nature of that kind of banking relationship is such that it tends to be a very personal, one-on-one connection. So I can predict, and usually be accurate, that that customer kept working with that person at the bank over the years, even though the person graduated up from branch manager and moved forward in the organization. That customer still has the access to that senior vice president, still has social connections with him, and still brings all of his banking business through that person. One time when I was training an advanced interviewing program, I asked the group, "Is that the case with you, that there are some people that you brought to the bank twenty years ago who still find a way to connect with you?" The answer, of course, was yes. So we established that these people were still invited to the customer's parties, cookouts, kids' birthday parties, and what not. Each person I was training had somebody who fell into that category, and a couple of people had quite a few people who fell into that category.

I said to them, "Okay, I want you to write down the name of the person in that category and the name of his company." They pulled out their notebooks and wrote the names down: Joe Jones of the Acme Wholesale Meat Company.

Now, here is a customer that they had been working with for twenty years. So I asked them a series of questions about that customer.

If I asked them things about that customer on a very basic social level, they knew the answer right away. "Does Joe Jones like to go fishing?" "Oh sure, he loves to go fishing." But if I ask about the customer's business, questions about what is going to be happening in this person's professional life, there's a huge gap. "How is Joe Jones maintaining a competitive edge?" "What is the next big trend in the meat packing business?" "Who are Joe's main competitors that he has to deal with right now?" "Who does he see as competition in the future?" No answers, no idea, no information about Joe Jones. They knew the names of his kids, but they didn't really know what he's likely to be using the money they're lending him for—or at least, they don't know what he's thinking about doing six months from now, or next year, or the year after that.

All of a sudden, very early on in the program, these senior VP's realized that they, supposedly the most experienced "salespeople" in the organization, simply did not know the answers to these fundamental questions. By that point, they were more willing to listen to some strategies that would help them get that information. That is what I want to share with you now.

If there's even a chance that you have a similar knowledge gap about what something your own best customer is dealing with in terms of maintaining a competitive edge in his industry, I'm going to ask you to try to study, and implement, what follows. Use this even if you've been selling for a long time, and even if you feel sure you know some of the people at your key accounts pretty well. Remember, in today's economy, knowing someone on a social level is not a meaningful barrier against your own competition's poaching on that account. You have to commit to knowing more than you currently do about the business challenges your customer encounters every day, and to developing an ongoing dossier of information about that person.

We've seen how the information we get from people improves with the time and quality of the relationship. We've also seen how the information gathering is critical to the sales process. Remember this model?

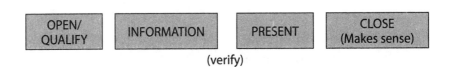

(verify)

I want to draw your attention once again to that verification substep that comes between the information and presentation steps. In actuality, we can spend quite a lot of time verifying what we have learned about the person and the institution before we ever attempt to present or close something within one of our key accounts. In fact, it's at the verification stage, the part of the process where we allow the other person to correct us, that we really build the relationship and enhance the quality of our insights on what's happening in the other person's world. It might even make more sense to look at the verification process as a series of conversations that serve as a checkpoint before we make any recommendation.

If we do a good job of verifying what we know about the other person's world, we are also doing a good job of building the relationship.

Building the relationship plays out best when we are building up trust and getting the person to do different things: giving us tours of their facility, taking tours of our facility, visiting to meet our people, or attending some kind of event we're hosting. The locale has to change, and more than that, the sense of investment in the other person has to change. There has to be an increased sense of involvement and credibility so that they can trust enough to share information with us about what they are doing. By the same token, once that feeling of credibility is in place, we're going to be in a better position to figure out what's really going on. We're going to reach a point where we can say to the other person, "Listen, just between you and me, what do you think is going to happen with this?" We'll get an honest answer, because we've been working consistently, over time, to confirm all of our assumptions about the account. If we do that in several different ways, and in different settings, it will pay off.

■ ■ ■

We have to work at this, though, because the process of verifying those assumptions does not play out automatically for us. In fact, our instinct usually points us in the opposite direction. We tend to assume we've done a better job of finding out about the other person's world than we actually have. Did you ever get out of a meeting and say to yourself, standing there in the parking lot, "Oh, I forgot to ask about X. Oh, I forgot to say Y. Oh, I forgot to check with him about Z."

Well, guess what? That happens to the prospect as well. He will leave the meeting and then he will think, as he walks down the hallway (and at the very minute you're standing in the parking lot), "Ah, I forgot to tell him X," or "Oh, I forgot to say Y," or "He'd need to know about Z."

As it happens, there are four possible reasons why the customer (or any customer) might have omitted critical information like that.

- He simply forgot.

- He ran out of time.

- He didn't think it was relevant.

- He didn't trust you.

Actually, looking at the list, probably number four is the most meaningful reason to consider, at least for our purposes as salespeople working in a key account setting. We have to remember: The customer is under no legal obligation to completely open up his business to you, especially early on in the relationship. As a general rule, the quality of the information we get reflects the current quality of the relationship. If we're getting bad information, it means we still have work to do in the relationship.

How do you get people to trust you enough to give you the information you want to know? It's a perpetual challenge, especially in the key account environment. You are constantly meeting new people. The truth is, it may take several conversations to get somebody to really open up to you. Everything hinges on your ability as a salesperson to first establish and then reinforce your credibility. Obviously, the commercial that you learned about in Chapter 62 will play a role here. Once you are in the interview, the intelligence and relevance of the questions you pose will be, during that session, your primary means of demonstrating that you are in fact worthy of trust. You have to become a great interviewer.

Start by making a lifelong commitment to learning what great interviewers do. One very easy way to do this is to pay particular attention to interviewers who already have the skill of building trust instantly. They are easier to model than you may think. All you have to do is make a commitment to study, on a professional level, the strategies used by the best hosts of interview programs on television and radio. I'm thinking about people like Oprah Winfrey or Barbara Walters.

These expert interviewers consistently start good conversations with people they may only have known for a few minutes, and they do it without overwhelming the person or monopolizing the conversation. They build up trust in a heartbeat, and they do it in front of an audience of millions. After all, isn't that what we are really after, the ability to bond quickly with someone and get the person to open up and give us the information we want, with a few very carefully and intelligently placed questions? Well, how does that happen? How do we lead the conversation without overwhelming it? What do Oprah and Barbara do that we should be doing?

Well, the number one thing that good interviewers do is always sound interested. Think about it: They can't possibly always be deeply interested in every one of the hundreds of people they interview over the course of the year, but somehow they manage to come across as deeply involved, caring, and engaged. That has to do with the eye contact they establish with the people they're talking to. Watch that eye contact sometime and see what you discover. Great interviewers strike an extraordinary balance with their gaze: it's direct, it's connected, it's even a little intense—but at the same time, their gaze somehow doesn't register as *too* intense. It's not as if they're staring the person down. They use their gaze to focus directly, powerfully, and intermittently on the person they're talking to. There's a certain power to the gaze of a great interviewer; they use that power to broadcast the message: "I'm connected to you, and I'm really interested in what you're telling me."

There are also nonverbal and semiverbal messages that great interviewers send while the other person is talking. They nod their heads to affirm that they "get" what the person has just shared; they raise their eyebrows as if to say, "Absolutely." They also make little noises like "mm-hmm" and "uh-huh"—these are all conversational supports that encourage the other person to open up, and reinforce the unspoken message: "I'm really listening. This is the most important thing that I'm doing right now." You know what? At the moment they send that message, they really mean it. That's what makes them great interviewers.

This sounds like a trivial point, but in fact, it is quite important from the point of view of the conversational dynamics that occur when you initiate conversation.

(An interesting side note: Social scientists who investigate group dynamics have found that one of the most important people in a group meeting is the person who plays the role of offering only nonverbal or low-level verbal assurances that it's okay to keep talking. That person ends up playing a really critical role in the decision-making processes of groups during business and policy meetings. If the group is going to make the best decisions, people have to be able to share their insights, and the process by which people end up feeling comfortable doing that is extremely important to the development of a sense of a cohesive group identity. The person who has that special role actually ends up being a really pivotal player in the meeting, even though he may not appear to have played much of a role in the ultimate content of the decision.)

■ ■ ■

The verbal and nonverbal messages above are ones you might find on a national television program. In the context of a sales meeting, one of the very strongest nonverbal signals I can send is taking notes. That's an even more direct way to get the message across: "I'm listening. This is important, this is the whole reason I'm here—to pay attention to what you're saying." That really does get people to open up and start sharing things with you. Try it!

When I take notes while the customer is talking, this suggests two things. First, "I am here on a professional assignment that I take seriously" (which puts me, paradoxically, in control of the exchange, even though someone else is doing the talking). Second, "I am here for you and your concerns, and I have put everything else on hold."

At the same time, I have to be careful. Let's say I'm talking to somebody, and that person is sharing some confidential information that is quite sensitive. What happens? The whole tonality is different when the person is discussing those issues. The physical posture of the person will change, he might lean in toward me a little bit. I see all that, and I hear this: "By the way, there are going to be huge changes in such and such an area, but nobody knows about this yet, so don't tell anybody."

Well, I do not want to write *that* down. In fact, my signal must be that I respect the person's confidence enough to stop writing. I want to make it absolutely clear that I recognize the extra importance of the fact the person has just shared.

The pad that you use to take notes, by the way, can send important nonverbal signals as well. You can use that pad as a bridge to the other person, perhaps by placing it on the table and drawing pictures and diagrams so you can get the other person's feedback. If a person is leaning in and commenting on what you've drawn or written, or perhaps has even picked up a pen and made changes of his own to the diagram, that is all the better.

My experience is that, for salespeople, the very best way to get the person to open up is to pull out the pad and pen (without asking for permission to do so), establish good but not aggressive eye contact, and take notes like crazy, using the notepad as a prop that occasionally elicits feedback from the other person. This is an intriguing way of leading the conversation while putting the other person in a superior social position. If you get really good at alternating between connecting with the person to establish eye contact, and taking notes, you can try the advanced version of this, which is to keep an eye on the person with your peripheral vision and monitor whether or how the person's body language changes when he thinks you're not looking. As I say, though, this is something you'll pick up over time. While you're still honing your skills, you should just alternate between solid, supportive, "I'm here and this is really interesting" eye contact and focused note taking.

ASK SIMPLE QUESTIONS

Notice that the really great interviewers do *little* of the talking because they find ways, both verbal and nonverbal, to get the other person to do most of the talking in a focused way. The direction of the conversation is not haphazard, but it's also not robotic. There's a clear understanding of what the interviewer wants to cover, but at the same time, if some new piece of information comes up, the interviewer knows how to explore that fully before moving on.

If the conversation does not involve the other person, it wasn't a good interview!

The main part of my job as an interviewer is to get the other person involved in the discussion. The second part of the job supports that main objective: I have to begin with easy questions.

Asking people easy questions is a great way to draw them in. Asking people hard questions is a great way to turn them off.

Let me give you an example of a hard question that intimidates people and will freeze up the atmosphere. Early on in the meeting, assume my very first question is, "Mr. Prospect, if you had a magic wand and could create the sales training program of your dreams, what would it look like?"

Well, that's an example of a very hard question to ask at the beginning of a meeting. Unless the person is very late in the IMP stage, he probably hasn't done the research and evaluation necessary to come anywhere close to being able to give an intelligent answer to that question. (Even if the person *is* late in the IMP stage, why is he going to instantly share all of that information with me right off the bat, on my very first question, at the very first meeting?)

Let's think pragmatically. We control the flow, right? People respond in kind, right? That means I have to think about what kind of answer I'm likely to generate with my question. In the real world, the answer that is going to come back is very likely to be something I really can't do anything with. Suppose the person says, "Gee, if I had a magic wand, you know what? I'd use it to create a free training program. That's the kind of thing that I'd be interested in—something that I didn't have to pay for." It could be an awkward moment!

So those are the hard questions. We want to avoid questions that demand a lot of the other person or that go in directions we can't do anything about. We want to start with easy questions.

If I want to have a conversation, I have a road map that I follow, with easy questions that will move me forward in the discussion. The first thing that we talk about is *the other person and his department.*

Ask Simple Questions About . . . the other person and his department, and how what this individual does fits into the company as a whole.

I am, by definition, interested in his role and the role of his department in the organization and the structure of his department. There is a lot of good information that I can uncover there, and since people, as a general rule enjoy talking about themselves, these are very likely to be easy questions. (If you haven't already asked about the person's career history, this is the perfect place to do so.)

Let's say I am talking to the head of marketing. Well, I want to find out how many people work in the marketing department. If the answer is two, that suggests something about that person's authority and power. On the other hand, if the answer is twenty-five, that is a very different picture. By asking about the structure of the department and about the role that the department has within the organization, I am really going to hear about the internal customers. I am going to find out which customers this department supports within the larger organization. By the way, these are other potential leads for me if I have to move on to another account strategy. That is a relatively easy question to ask. It will give me a lot of information and it is a good way to begin the discussion.

In fact, sometimes the customers are so accustomed to getting a question about department structure that they even have a handy organizational chart that they will hand out so I can get all the information about what their department does in a permanent form. That's great! I don't even have to write it down. Sometimes, though, they will not have such a chart handy, so I will draw out the organizational chart as I understand it, and show it to my contact for feedback. If the conversation ended right then and there, if the person was called away to a meeting for some reason, at minimum my notes now have the structure of that department and some kind of sense about who the other people and departments that person's department serves are.

Now, in asking these questions, I do not want to ask immediately about things that have a connection to my product, but I am going to ask about the company. I am going to ask them how sales are in the company. Who do they sell to? How many customers do they have? Where are these customers? How much new business? What is the relationship between new business and old business? Is there any seasonal component to it? How are sales now? How does that compare to how they were in the past? How does it compare to their expectations for where they were going to be this year?

Let me tell you why these questions are important. No matter what product I am selling, if sales in that company are about to go up or have gone up, that will impact everything that happens in that department. Not only will they have more money for purchasing things, but they will be buying different kinds of things and doing that buying for a different reason. The same thing, of course, works in reverse. I should know if sales are dramatically lower than expectations or dramatically lower than this time last year. Also, on occasion, the customers they list may end up being leads for me.

So the first point on my road map of easy questions is the person, the department, and how this individual role fits into the company as a whole. I am going to ask in a general way about how business is and what the sales trend is, but I am going to avoid the temptation to jump into some kind of presentation about why the person should buy from me. I don't know enough yet to make that kind of recommendation. Instead, I'm going to move forward to the next point on my roadmap of easy questions.

Building on what I already know, I am going to use the information I have just uncovered to confirm whatever I can about the structure of the organization.

Ask Simple Questions About . . . the structure of the larger organization.

You can see, I think, how the first set of easy questions dovetails nicely into this second group of easy questions. How does this person's division deliver what it delivers to the rest of the organization? Who are the internal customers? What is the overall structure of the company?

Just as we wanted to get (or create) a simplified visual display of the person's immediate surroundings (the department), we also want to get (or create) a chart that shows us exactly how the company as a whole breaks down.

And throughout this process, of course, I want to consider asking questions such as: How are decisions typically made at such-and-such a level? Where are the formal lines of authority and, just as important, where are the informal lines of authority? Who does my contact know best in these other work groups, and which parts of the company are unfamiliar to him?

Once we get the lay of the land of the organization's dimensions, we're going to hold on to that information and mentally file away its main points as we branch out to deal with other people. After all, this contact's perception of how the organization is structured, and how things really get done, may be radically different from someone else's perceptions! I want to be able to keep coming back to my notes and compare the differing explanations I get about how the company as a whole works and how it is structured. Sometimes, the divergences will tell me a whole lot about the differing agendas of the various people involved.

Can you see how focusing on these two initial topics—my contact's role and the structure of the organization—actually give me very important information, yet are, at the same time, quite easy for the other person to respond to? This is the way we want to escalate the conversation. If we just barged in the door and started demanding to know what kind of criteria they use to judge their vendors, we wouldn't get the same level of connection, and the information we uncovered wouldn't be as reliable.

Next on the agenda, we're going to ask the person about his company's critical suppliers.

Ask Simple Questions About . . . the organization's most important suppliers.

To be more specific, I want to validate my own assumptions regarding the company's suppliers, not just my immediate competitors. In fact, I don't really want to start with the competition. (Again, we're talking about easy questions.) Instead, I'd rather find out about their other relationships, and preferably about their most important strategic partners. Do they buy consulting services? Do they have shipping partnerships? Do they have customs partnerships? Are there software partnerships that are strategically important to the business? How does this organization partner with other people and organizations that aren't in my industry? (Notice that this is an easy variation on the question I eventually want to ask, namely, "How does this organization partner with people who sell what I sell?") Which organizations are the most important to this company? What are the criteria? How do they go about selecting people? Of course, one of the main things I have learned is: "Who is likely to make the next decision?" How and why the last decision was made is something I have to address fully at some point. I may not be able to get all the information from this person, but I do have to figure it out somewhere along the line. One classic strategy for escalating the discussion, of course, is to pose a question that I know my contact can't possibly answer, and then try to identify who else in the organization could answer it for us.

Eventually, when I build the right rapport and ask the right questions about suppliers, I'm going to get a sense of the important areas that my contact knows about, and how those relationships are initiated. (By the way, some of those suppliers are in fact going to be leads for me even though some of them are going to be competitors, too.)

I am also going to learn, beyond everything else, what the organization's buying patterns are. How they like to buy, who is involved in the decision, whether the person I am talking to was historically involved in that decision the last time around, and so on. All of that is very important information.

These are among the questions I am going to ask somebody else in the organization to answer if my contact does not know. Obviously, I am going to work my way through the whole organization in search of that kind of information, and I'm going to be working my way toward those elephant questions, making sure to ask the easiest versions of the question first, and working my way up to more difficult questions like these: Why aren't you working with us? Have you ever thought about working with somebody like us? Who are you using now? Who were you using before? Why did you leave? What made you decide to pick them? Have you called anybody else? Are you looking at anybody else? These are all the kinds of questions I *eventually* want to pose, but I have to remember that I'm going to get the best quality of information if I start with the easier questions, establish rapport with those simple questions, and then slowly work my way up to the more difficult questions.

(Note: Long years of experience have taught me that I am far better off asking a question about the how or why of the decision to work with a vendor, than I am asking, "Are you the decision maker for such and such an area?" People have a way of magnifying their own level of importance when you ask them if they have decision-making authority—but if you ask them about the how and the why of a past decision, their actual level of knowledge, influence, and authority becomes immediately obvious.)

Based on your own assessment of the situation, you may choose not to address the potentially difficult questions such as, "How did you choose such-and-such a competitor?" until after you explore the final point on the "easy" question roadmap. Once you have explored the role of the person and the department, the structure of the company, and the key suppliers, you should ask about the company's competition.

Ask Simple Questions About . . . the organization's perceived competition.

This is another questioning category that will tell you a great deal about the person's level of influence and authority within the organization. Mid-level and low-level decision makers will be very likely to give you superficial, incomplete, or totally meaningless answers when you say "Who do you consider to be your number one competitor?" Senior level executives, on the other hand, will often be so inspired by the question, that they launch into a sustained lecture on the industry and its players. You may be surprised to learn that a division of your company considers itself to have internal competition from another corner of the company, or from a distributor. Write it all down, unless of course your contact prefers that you not record the information.

A very few key top-level executives will consider a completely honest answer to the question, "Who is the number one competitor, in your view?" to fall under the category of privileged internal information, and will either turn the question around and pose it to you, or politely decline the opportunity to go into specifics. Do not challenge these people.

Instead, move on to a generic, and unthreatening, version of the same question. I use a variation that just about anyone at the top level of a company is highly motivated to answer. It sounds like this: "How do you hold on to a competitive edge in an industry like this?" That's a very important question, one you should make a point of posing to everyone of any importance. The answer you get will tell you a great deal about the way the person looks at the industry, the company, the company's assets, and its current challenges.

This is the last of the four easy question categories. Of course, some of the competitors that I uncover by asking questions in this fourth spot on the road map are going to end up being leads for me. Notice that every easy questioning category can, if used intelligently, help me produce new business elsewhere.

If I follow this sequence at the beginning of my interviewing and information-gathering phase, I am going to have a much better, fuller picture of the people, structure, and challenges within this particular key account. At the very same time, I will show a genuine interest in the person, demonstrate my ability to ask pertinent questions, and show myself and my company in the best light as a consultative professional who is genuinely curious about where the company is going. As a result, I will get more of the blanks filled in, and I will get more and better internal referrals within the key account.

YOUR SECRET WEAPON FOR EXPANDING YOUR NETWORK

I think the most serious problem salespeople have when it comes to selling into their key accounts may well be the problem of complacency. Sometimes we become so comfortable dealing with a certain familiar contact, and selling a certain product mix, that we forget that we have an obligation to expand our influence and our network of contacts within the account.

In this, the final chapter of this book, I want to share with you a secret weapon for overcoming this complacency and for identifying other contacts and potential markets within the account. It's a weapon that you already use every single day. It requires no special training for proper use, other than the simple ideas I'm going to share with you. This weapon will, if used properly, get you in the door with more people than you're talking to right now.

The weapon is, of course, your telephone.

How can you have more and better telephone conversations that will expand your presence within the accounts that buy from you on a regular basis? I want to emphasize that you should use the ideas that follow in collaboration with the principles for face-to-face discussions that appear elsewhere in this book. For now, though, I want you to start thinking of your telephone as a neglected resource in identifying and building relationships with people you should know more about within accounts that buy from you on a regular basis.

Let's look at the different scenarios under which that could happen.

SCENARIO #1: You don't yet have internal referrals from a primary contact you don't see in person very often . . .

If you've fallen into the trap of having regular conversations with one and only one person within the account, I want to urge you to find ways to develop new contacts through that person. One good way to do that is by using the telephone. Of course, it's unlikely that you're going to get good results by simply calling the person up and saying, "Listen, I'm afraid you may end up getting fired or may decide to move on to another company, so just as a safety precaution, could you please introduce me to the four or five most important people at your organization?"

A somewhat more intelligent and rewarding phone call will sound like this:

> *Customer:* Mike Customer here.
>
> *You:* Hey there, Mike. This is Bart Dillon at Unicroyd Industries. I was just thinking of you. *(Stop talking.)*
>
> *Customer:* Is that right? What were you thinking about?
>
> *You:* Actually, I was thinking that it had been a while since you and I got together face-to-face. I decided that I wanted to fulfill my New Year's resolution, which is to spend more face time with my best customers. Is there any chance I could take you out to lunch next Tuesday around noon?
>
> *Customer:* Well, that day is full but could we meet for lunch Wednesday at 1:00 P.M.? I'm always up for being taken out to lunch.
>
> *You:* No problem. I'll mark it down. Looking forward to seeing you.
>
> *Customer:* Great.

If you make this call, in roughly this way, hitting all the marks that I've laid out here, and that includes opening the call with that strangely evocative phrase, "I was just thinking of you," followed by silence, you will find that current customers will in fact respond quite positively to such a meeting.

And why shouldn't you meet face-to-face more often with your primary contact at your key account? If you're pressed on the reason or goal for the meeting, you should say that you're interested in finding out what kind of projects the person's working on and what major plans he is pursuing in the month, quarter, or year ahead.

When you actually show up for the lunch meeting, of course, there will be a certain level of social pleasantry to the exchange. But that's not all that's going to happen here. While you're at the restaurant, you're going to ask Mike to take you on a tour of his facility, either right after lunch or at some point in the near future. In other words if you haven't yet had the chance to walk around his or her office, factory, or showroom, this is the time that you're going to ask for that guided tour. (Don't ask for this over the phone, but *do* ask for it while you're face-to-face with your customer. Ideally, you should pick a restaurant that's close to the facility where your customer works. Nine times out of ten your customer will agree and maybe even be a little flattered by the attention.)

During this informal walkthrough, you're going to distribute as many business cards as you can to the all people that you meet. And by "everyone" I mean everyone, from the receptionist to the president of the company as well as everyone in between. You're going to ask your primary contact to introduce you to as many people as possible, and you're going to ask each of those people what they do and what their job function is. At an appropriate opportunity, you're going to praise Mike, your primary contact, in plausible ways, and in front of the people he works with. You're going to ask as many questions about the factory, the working processes, and the overall working day that you possibly can.

Of course as you're handing out your business cards, you're also going to be collecting business cards. These days, everybody's business card contains an e-mail address. At the end of the day, or at the very latest before lunch tomorrow, you're going to follow through with each and every one of the people that you met in person and send them a personalized e-mail message, thanking them for taking the opportunity to chat with you the other day.

Before you leave the facility, however, you're going to ask your primary contact about internal referrals to the organization where you are already selling into. You're going to ask who you should be talking to either at this facility or at some other facility who might also be able to use your products or services. You're going to stop talking at the end of that meeting and find out exactly what Mike has to offer once you've made the request.

This may feel a little uncomfortable, but it's definitely worth doing—and definitely preferable to not asking for referrals. Actually, it only seems uncomfortable to you, because you're expecting that Mike will somehow resent the fact that you're trying to identify other opportunities for business. In the real world, there's no reason whatsoever for Mike to resent that, and he's probably expecting it, knowing as he does that you're a salesperson.

One of our top salespeople, Jeff Goldberg, told me a story once about a meeting with one of his customers where he asked for precisely this kind of a referral. At the end of a tour through the customer's operations (that he'd set up by phone), and just as he was getting ready to wrap up his session in his contact's office, Jeff looked his contact in the eye and asked, "Who else do you think I should be talking to in this company about sales training?" There was a weird little pause and then Jeff's contact, whose name was John, said, "Well, I guess you might want to hook up with Erma at some point. Erma Johnson has a team of about one hundred salespeople who report to her over in our Buffalo office."

It was at this stage that Jeff did something that really set him apart from most of the other salespeople that his contacts will run into during the course of the year. Jeff smiled, thanked his contact for that information, and then said, "Would you mind calling Erma right now just to let her know that I'm going to be in touch with her?" (As it turned out, the contact was more comfortable sending an e-mail message, which was also fine with Jeff.)

The following morning, Jeff called Erma, using strategies you're about to learn, to try to set an appointment with her to discuss her sales training program. She agreed to a meeting, and when Jeff walked into her office, a few days later, she greeted him with a warm handshake and a very strange opening remark. She said, "Jeff, I want you to know, that I've absolutely no interest whatsoever in buying any sales training from you for at least the next eighteen months."

Jeff was a little taken aback by this and he asked the natural question that most salespeople would ask in that situation, which was, "Okay, then can I ask why you agreed to meet with me?"

Without batting an eye, Erma told him, "The reason I'm meeting with you is simply that John e-mailed me and asked me to sit down with you. That's it. There really is no interest whatsoever in working with DEI at this stage."

Not wanting to appear too standoffish, Jeff suggested they sit down anyway and just talk about what was happening in her department. Sure enough, that's what they did . . . and believe it or not, Jeff managed to establish a Next Step, coming out of that meeting with a proposal for an auxiliary series of training programs even though Erma had said at the outset of the meeting that she wasn't interested in discussing any such thing. Do you know that he ended up closing a $25,000 deal with that woman?

There are several lessons to learn from that story.

- No. 1, The first lesson I get is that Jeff made the right decision to call John in the first place and ask to take a tour of his facility. (Again, the telephone is a great secret tool.)

- No. 2, Jeff did exactly the right thing in asking directly for referrals at the end of that meeting.

- No. 3, Jeff did exactly the right thing in asking his primary contact to make a phone call to the people to whom he was being referred.

(Never mind that the contact decided not to make a phone call but sent an e-mail. The fact that Jeff asked for it was enough to deliver the results that Jeff wanted, namely John contacting Erma.)

- ☐ No. 4, Jeff was absolutely right in calling the next day to schedule an appointment with Erma.

- ☐ No. 5, Jeff was absolutely right in sticking with his plan to sit down with Erma and find out what was going on in her department despite the fact that she gave him the upfront message that she had no interest whatsoever in buying.

- ☐ And finally, No. 6, Jeff's tenacity and good spirits combined to make Items 1 to 5 play out positively in a nonconfrontational way with each of these critical contacts.

All too often, I meet salespeople who tell me that they're uncomfortable asking current customers to meet with them, and uncomfortable asking current customers for referrals. This is, to put it bluntly, balderdash. Most people you talk to during the course of the day will in fact know that you sell for a living, and they will not be shocked that a salesperson actually asks for referrals at the end of a meeting. So don't let them down. Ask directly for the referrals, and if you get any, ask if the person will make a call right then and there on your behalf.

SCENARIO #2: Once you've received a referral from the customer at your key account . . .

Here's what Jeff's call to Erma sounded like. Notice that it breaks down into four components.

> **Part 1**—Attention Statement: "Hello, Erma?"
>
> Erma: (Any response.)
>
> **Part 2**—Identification Statement: "This is Jeff Goldberg calling you from DEI. Did John tell you that I was going to call?"

(Notice that we are identifying ourselves and then instantly asking a question that we can handle the answer to. If the answer is "Yes, John did say you'd be calling," we can say, "Great, what did he tell you about our meeting?" If she says, "No, John didn't say anything about your calling," then we can say, "Well, let me tell you what John and I discussed . . .")

Part 3—Identification Statement, continued: "Well I'm not sure if you've ever heard of us, but DEI Management Group is a global sales and training organization that was started in 1979 by my boss, Steve Schiffman. We cover training and appointment-making, prospect management, and high efficiency selling. We've worked with John on projects such as A, B, and C."

Part 4—The Reason for the Call: "The reason John thought you and I ought to be talking together is that I just delivered a program for him that helps him to increase his total appointments by fifteen percent after just one week from the time that we implemented the program. I'd love to get together with you and show you the program I put together for him. Could we meet next Tuesday at 2:00 p.m.?"

Of course there's a lot more we could get into on how to handle the possible objections that may come up as a result of that discussion. For now, just focus on the fact that we're using John's name, with his permission, and we're appealing to the success of the program that we delivered for John. The meeting to discuss the program we put together for John really is the reason for our call to Erma. And specifically, whether we can meet with Erma on Tuesday at 2:00 P.M. is the reason for the call. (Remember: We control the flow!)

That opening line, "Did John tell you that I was going to call," serves as a kind of icebreaker for the discussion, so we can move forward and focus on one thing and one thing only: The appointment with Erma next Tuesday at 2:00 P.M. When we make that request for a specific date and time we're really throwing out the ball to Erma and finding out if she's willing to play ball with us. In this case, she was willing to play ball with Jeff, but only because he had the endorsement and the referral from John's e-mail. (Of course, she also would have agreed to the meeting had John called her, rather than e-mailing her.)

SCENARIO #3: Calling Without a Referral

It's a tricky diplomatic situation when you know you've been boxed in by a contact who does not want to give you referrals to other people in the organization. At that point, you have a couple of different options. The first option is to make the call directly to the people you are able to identify through research on the Web, the local library, perusing the company's annual report, or by any number of other sources.

A slightly less risky approach, however, is to elicit the help of your sales manager and have him accompany you on any visits to other contacts within the account. If there's any static about the meeting, you can appeal to the authority of a higher power. ("I didn't want to go over your head—my sales manager made me call that person. Heck, he even insisted on coming along on the meeting.") You will find that most sales managers will be happy to help you expand your influence within the account in this way.

The call you make is basically going to break down along very similar lines to the call that Jeff made to Erma. The only difference is that it's going to be lacking the reference point of the specific internal contact and instead will refer to the work you've done in the organization as a whole. Take a look:

> **Part 1**—Attention Statement: "Hi, is this Darryl Bigshot."
> Nonreferral: (Any response.)

> **Part 2**—Identification Statement: "Well, I'm not sure if you've ever heard of us, but DEI Management Group is a global sales and training organization that was started in 1979 by my boss, Steve Schiffman. Have you ever heard of Stephan Schiffman?

> (Again, this is a question that I can handle no matter which answer the person gives. If the person says yes he's heard of Steven Schiffman or he's heard of my company, then I can say, "Great, what have you heard about Steve?" If the person says "No,

I've never heard of him before," I can proceed with the rest of my identification statement.)

Part 3—Identification Statement, continued. "We cover training and appointment-making, prospect management, and high-efficiency selling. And we've worked with your company on projects A, B, and C."

Part 4—The Reason for the Call: "The reason for my call is that I'd like to swing by this next Tuesday at 2:00 P.M. with my sales manager, so we can show you some of the work that we've been doing. Would that be a good time to meet, next Tuesday at 2:00 P.M.?"

Again, it's important to remember that this is just a bare-bones outline for the conversation. It's quite possible that the call will go in different directions and it's a mistake to think the script that I've provided for you is a magic wand or special incantation that will automatically generate meetings with other people. It is, however, highly effective as a map or outline for a call to set up the First Appointment.

I've covered just the barest outlines of an effective calling campaign here. For more information on how to perfect your calling campaign, please see my book, *Cold Calling Techniques (That Really Work!).*

SIX REASONS TO FIGHT FOR A NEXT STEP

From D.E.I. Sales Training (www.dei-sales.com)

In selling, a Next Step is tangible evidence that someone is working with you. It's not a gut feeling that the person is interested in working with you, but proof of that interest.

At D.E.I Sales Training, where I work, we believe that interest is demonstrated by action. That action takes the form of an agreement to meet with you, speak to you, or do something for you, typically within the next two weeks. This is the Next Step.

SIX REASONS TO FIGHT FOR A NEXT STEP

Reason #1: It Shortens Your Selling Cycle

At the end of a sales meeting, most salespeople say, "I'll call you in a week or two." They end up wasting all kinds of time playing phone tag. Why not set the Next Step while you're still face-to-face? You can save one to three weeks between each meeting, and perhaps as much as a month off your overall sales cycle. (You can save time every day by avoiding phone tag, too.)

Reason #2: Territory Management

Once you know you are meeting again with this client, you can set up another appointment in the area. You can work in advance to set up these meetings. This contact may be more likely to meet with you at hard-to-fill time slots (8:00 A.M., 4:00 P.M.) than someone you have no rapport or history with.

Reason #3: Time Management

Fact of sales life: The proposal that's due sometime next week will probably slip to the bottom of your priority list. The proposal that's due because of a meeting you've scheduled for next Tuesday at 2:00 P.M. will be less likely to slip. Find out exactly when it's due so you know when to "do" it. Why? Because there are three things you should always make a conscious effort to schedule: Meetings with prospects, work you have to do before a meeting with a prospect, and prospecting time.

Reason #4: You'll Know Who to Follow Up With

Let's say it's a busy month. Maybe you have twenty First Appointments in a busy month. Say that seven of them don't go anywhere because you get a clear no or the person is obviously unqualified. If you don't ask for a Next Step, at the end of the first meeting, that means thirteen people are in "call-me-next-week-sometime" mode. Come to think of it, you also have thirteen people like that from last month, and thirteen from the month before that. But suppose you've only got time for five quality proposals this month. Who do you focus on? Well, if you regularly ask for a Next Step, you know exactly who you should write a proposal for—the people who agree to a Next Step! Remember, interest is demonstrated by action. You are prioritizing people who agree to Next Steps because at least they agreed to see you again. The others, when asked, didn't agree to see you. So here's the question: If they didn't agree to see you, what makes you think they'll buy from you?

Reason #5: You'll Send the Right Message

Translation: Your time is valuable, too. Consider this: We teach people how to buy from us. So we don't want to say, "When are you free?" but rather, "I've got a slot at 11:00 A.M. on Tuesday, does that work?" Sending the "When are you free?" message is professional suicide. Why would you want to send someone the message, "I'll travel two hours out of my way to spend two minutes with you"?

Reason #6: You Worked Too Damn Hard to Set Up the Appointment in the First Place

You've made a sizeable time investment to set this up, drive out, and meet with the prospect. Why walk away from that without a commitment?

SIXTEEN WAYS TO ASK FOR A NEXT STEP

From D.E.I. Sales Training (www.dei-sales.com)

1. When You Want to Get Corrected

(This is probably the simplest and most effective Next Step strategy.)

"I think this meeting went well."

"Here's why I think it went well. I see a possible match between what you're trying to accomplish and what we do."

"So, let me tell you what I think we should do."

"I want to come back here on Tuesday at 2:00 P.M. and show you an outline of how we might be able to work together based on what we've talked about today. Does that make sense?"

2. When You've Hit a Technical Obstacle

"Let me come back here on Tuesday at 2:00 P.M. and introduce your tech person to my tech person."

3. When You Want to Escalate the Sale

"I get the feeling I should meet your boss. Why don't you and I meet with him on Tuesday at 2:00 P.M.?"

4. When You Want to Escalate the Sale (Variation)

"I really get the feeling your boss ought to meet my boss. Let's set up a meeting. How's Tuesday at 2:00 P.M.?"

5. When You Want to Gain or Regain Access to Key People

"Let's meet with your team for an hour, so we can all work together to build the proposal for you. How's Tuesday at 2:00 P.M.?"

6. When You Want to Reassure the Prospect

"Let's have a meeting with Happy Customer. You really ought to talk to him. How's Tuesday at 2:00 P.M.?"

7. When You Want to Position Yourself as a Virtual Employee

"I've got an idea. Why don't I talk to your team about what they're doing . . . and do a little free consulting for you? I'll give you my analysis. We should really set up a date for me to report back to you. How's Tuesday at 2:00 P.M.?"

8. When the Prospect Is Having Trouble Visualizing the Benefit of What You Sell

"I've got an idea. Why don't you come by and sit in on one of our programs/training sessions/other customer event. How's Tuesday at 8:00 A.M.?"

9. When You Want to Improve Your Relationship by Spending Time at a Neutral Site

"I've got an idea. We've got tickets for a special industry event/trade show, and I'd love for you to be there and see it. How's Tuesday night at 8:00 P.M.?"

10. When You Want to Exchange Access to Their People for Access to Your Product

"I've got an idea. Why don't I set up a demonstration for you and your boss so you can see how this product works. How's Tuesday at 2:00 P.M.?"

11. When You Want to Help Them Visualize How You Can Benefit Them

"I've got an idea. Why don't you come by and visit our facilities so you can see how we work and meet our key people. How's Tuesday at 2:00 P.M.?"

12. When You Want to Reassure Them That You Understand Why They're Different

"I've got an idea. Why don't I take a tour of your plant and see it first hand. How's Tuesday at 2:00?"

13. When You Want to Rescue a Fallback, a Dormant Lead

"I've been thinking about the plan we put together for you, and I'm not happy with it. I have a new plan that I want to show you. Can I come by Tuesday at 2:00 P.M.?"

14. When You Want to Rescue a Fallback, a Dormant Lead (Variation)

"I was just thinking of you. We really ought to get together again. Can I come by Tuesday at 2:00 P.M.?"

15. When You Want to Rescue a Fallback, a Dormant Lead (Variation)

"I'm going to be in the area, meeting with XYZ Company. We ought to get together again so I can see what you're doing. Can I come by Tuesday at 2:00 P.M.?"

16. When You Want to Rescue a Fallback, a Dormant Lead (Variation)

"I have an idea I want to discuss with you. Can I come by Tuesday at 2:00 P.M.?"

FINALLY, REMEMBER THIS …

Whatever the situation, you must make absolutely sure the Next Steps you suggest are:

- ▣ Clear
- ▣ Perceived as Helpful
- ▣ Easy to Agree To

EIGHT THINGS YOU CAN DO TO REIGNITE A RELATIONSHIP WITH A KEY ACCOUNT

From D.E.I. Sales Training (www.dei-sales.com)

Sometimes the opportunity for new business with a new decision maker materializes in one of our key accounts then "falls back" to inactive status. Here are some strategies for moving the person back into one of the active prospect categories.

1. Ask your primary contact, the one who is still working with you, to go to lunch with you. Get him or her to bring the "fallback" decision maker along to the lunch meeting. During lunch, ask the fallback decision maker if you did anything wrong. Stop talking and see what he or she says.

2. Call and say, "I was just thinking of you." Point out that you were going to be in the neighborhood to meet with Company X, and you want to get together on Tuesday at 2:00 to discuss a project you are working on elsewhere in the organization. (If possible, get your primary contact involved with the meeting as well.)

3. Invite the fallback contact to an upcoming training program or public event and simultaneously schedule a face-to-face meeting

or conference call to follow up in person after the event and see what the person thought of it.

4. Suggest to your primary contact that you do a small-scale pilot program, or deliver a sample of your product or service to a fallback contact within the account. Get his buy-in and endorsement of this idea. Call up the fallback contact and say, "I was talking to James over in the widget department, and he thinks I should do a free pilot program for your team. Can we meet and talk about it tomorrow morning at 8:00 P.M.?"

5. Brainstorm an idea with your primary contact that might help the fallback decision maker. Call the fallback decision maker and say, "I was talking to James, and we came up with an idea he thought we should all discuss with you. Can the three of us meet next Tuesday at 2:00 P.M.?"

6. Suggest to your primary contact that the fallback could benefit from talking to a current customer of yours. (Make sure this customer operates in an industry that does not compete with the key account you're trying to sell to.) Get the primary contact's buy-in on this idea. Call the fallback decision maker and say, "James and I were talking, and we thought you should be talking to Happy Customer of Mine. Can you and I do a conference call with this person on Tuesday at 2:00 P.M.?"

7. Mail an article with relevant business advice to the fallback decision maker. Include a nice handwritten note. Follow up by phone to see what the person thought of the article. Ask to meet this coming Tuesday at 2:00 P.M.; try to include your main contact in the meeting if at all possible.

8. Mail a copy of a book that you found helpful to the fallback decision maker. Include a nice handwritten note. Follow up by phone to see what the person thought of the book. Ask to meet this coming Tuesday at 2:00; try to include your main contact in the meeting if at all possible.

THIRTEEN PROVEN
SELLING PRINCIPLES

From D.E.I. Sales Training (www.dei-sales.com)

1. *The objective* of each step is to get to the Next Step.

2. *The definition* of selling is helping people do what they do better.

3. *No one "needs" us* or what we have to offer. If anyone did need us, they would have already called us.

4. *Our number one competitor* is the status quo, what the person or organization is already doing.

5. *Sell to the obvious* by asking how and why the person is already doing what he is doing.

6. *The sales process* is an extended conversation. We can control the flow of that conversation.

7. *The longer a sale takes* out of its normal sales cycle, the less likely it is to happen.

8. *The key to effective sales* is ratios, not numbers.

9. *All responses* we hear are in kind; all can be anticipated; all are likely to be told in stories.

10. *Seventy-five percent of the work* in the ideal sales process occurs prior to the proposal, or presentation, of your plan.

11. *Our close* should be a natural outgrowth of the sales process and sounds like this: "Makes sense to me. What do you think?"

12. *We want the prospect to decide to buy.* We don't want to have to sell to the prospect.

13. *We can predict future income* based on current activity.

TWELVE PROVEN TIME-MANAGEMENT PRINCIPLES FOR SALESPEOPLE

From D.E.I. Sales Training (www.dei-sales.com)

Are your salespeople using their available time wisely? They will be if they follow these twelve simple principles.

1. Start early each day. Give yourself time to wake up.

2. Assume everything takes longer than you think it will. You'll be right.

3. Assume everyone else will take longer than you think to get back to you. You'll be right.

4. Don't skimp on reading and thinking time, but don't pursue these activities during prime selling hours.

5. Assign the right number of minutes to every task on your list. Know how much time you intend to invest in a given activity.

6. Keep simplifying your filing system. Remember, if it doesn't work as a finding system, it's fatally flawed.

7. Break all tasks down to smaller, manageable tasks. Focus on first steps and very Next Steps. Track your progress on each item in a written log.

8. Be your own boss. Know your own weaknesses and hold yourself accountable. Give yourself appropriate rewards for completing important tasks that it may be difficult to motivate yourself to complete.

9. Know the difference between being busy and being productive. It's easy to be busy without being productive. For salespeople, *productive* means "moves me measurably closer to a commission." Here are the only four scenarios that qualify as a productive day:

   a. I scheduled a First Appointment with someone.

   b. I moved an existing prospect forward, as evidenced by that prospect's willingness to either sign a contract or set aside a specific date and time to talk to me within the next two weeks.

   c. I reached a current or former client (by making a phone call, sending out a mailing, sending a personalized e-mail, etc.).

   d. I did any combination of a, b, or c above.

   Anything else is not a productive day, only a busy day!

10. Cluster similar activities together. Yes, you'll be interrupted during the day. That doesn't mean that your priorities for the day should change in a heartbeat. Try to gather similar activities into the same chunk of the day.

11. Plan everything two weeks in advance. You should know, today, what your major priorities are going to be for each of the next ten business days.

12. Budget and monitor your daily, weekly, monthly, and yearly time commitments (in round numbers). Then take ten minutes

once a week, and compare what actually happened to what you wanted to happen in a given activity area. For instance, you have approximately 2,000 working hours to invest in any given year. How many of those hours should go to prospecting for new business? Settle on a number, then see how it breaks down when you divide it to correspond with daily, weekly, or monthly time investments. After a week of keeping track, do this ten-minute assessment once again. How does your reality compare to your projection? What should you be doing differently?

PROGRAMS AVAILABLE FROM D.E.I.

Founded by international sales consultant Stephan Schiffman, D.E.I. Franchise Systems has emerged as America's premier sales training franchise opportunity for three reasons:

- It is a powerful, globally recognized brand

- It is a proven sales improvement system that's delivered results to over 500,000 salespeople at 9,000 companies

- It is a "get-you-up-and-running-quick" management philosophy

D.E.I. franchisees receive world-class training, one-on-one territory matching, and ongoing support. Our package includes:

- 1,000 leads upon signing

- Exclusive territories

- A tested, replicated business model that allows you to be in business in four weeks.

Our philosophy is simple: The sooner you're up and running, the sooner you can see a return on your investment.

THE D.E.I. ADVANTAGE

- Proven selling systems that our trainers both use and deliver

- Stephan Schiffman, our president and founder, has more than one million books in print

- Schiffman's book and audiotape presence at Kinko's, Borders, Barnes & Noble, and Amazon.com has built our programs into a globally recognized brand

THE WORLD-CLASS SALES TRAINING AUTHORITY

With offices across the United States and around the world, D.E.I. Management Group ranks as America's training authority, boasting clients ranging from Fortune 500 companies to startups, and a franchisee network that is second to none.

Our client list is a powerful selling tool—it includes some of the best-known names in American business, including:

Aetna	AT&T
Blue Cross/Blue Shield	Boise Office Solutions
ChevronTexaco	Cox Communications
EMC	Federal Express
IBM	Merrill Lynch
Motorola	*The New York Times*
Sony	Waste Management

QUICK RAMP-UP

Our exclusive PowerStart (TM) training program gets our franchisees up and running with key concepts quickly. Our follow-through program is the best in the industry because we give our franchisees personal exposure and access to the most senior people in our organization.

We offer:

- Monthly Webinars with D.E.I. President

- Weekly business coaching conference calls with senior D.E.I. staff

- Weekly summaries of franchisee activity and networking opportunities

- Tri-monthly clinics with our senior D.E.I. Training Director

- Quarterly team continuing education/networking events

- Annual network convention

WHAT OUR FRANCHISEES SAY

- This is a great business; it's highly enjoyable and as businesses go, it can deliver a very good lifestyle, cash flow, and profits.

- The training and the system work. That may seem simple and taken for granted, but you'll only appreciate the strength of the system when you see the effects it has in a company.

- There is far less risk here than with many other businesses because you start with a selling system that is designed to protect you and help you succeed.

- Most new businesses are most exposed in the selling area. DEI has that taken care of from the start. Everything that the system predicts will happen and can be managed.

To request a franchise information kit, call us today at 1-800-224-2140!

Visit *www.dei-sales.com* for eLearning!
eLearning Courses
Concise online courses that help you improve critical selling and management skills. Most can be completed in less than twenty minutes!

Cold Calling Techniques
How to Get More Appointments
Don't Wait to Hear No
Getting to "Closed"—Prospect Management
High Efficiency Selling
Seven Make it Happen Questions You're Not Asking

Sixteen Keys to Getting More Appointments
The Monday Morning Meeting
The Top Ten Sales Mistakes (and How to Avoid Them)
Using Questions to Accelerate Sales

Visit *www.dei-sales.com* for webinars!
Webinars

LIVE one-on-one coaching with Stephan Schiffman . . . over the Internet! Check our site regularly for new online events. Topics include:

Getting Your Foot in the Door
Ask Questions, Get Sales
How to Be #1 on Your Sales Team
Closing Techniques That Really Work
The Art of Generating and Managing Leads

Index

Presenting/presentation, 39–40
four P's and, 53–56
gathering information before, 40–42, 84
in triangle model context, 78–79
Pressures, on decision makers, 149–50
Pricing, 16, 17. *See also* Discounts
Primary contact, defined, 4
Principles
of being right, 83–84
communication, 146–48
negotiating, 15–17
selling, 244–45
time-management, 246–48
Product knowledge, four P's and, 54, 56
Professional development, four P's and, 54–55, 56
Props, for communication, 144–45
Prospecting/prospects, 5. *See also*
Communication; Interviewing
customers; Number(s); Qualifying
balancing prospecting, 58–59
calling new referral, 232–34
calling without referral, 234–35
categorizing prospects, 162–64
defining prospects, 23–24
developing, 49–52
four P's and, 53–56
increasing, 59–62
major accounts, 120–21
"No" answers and, 60
prospecting defined, 53
prospect-to-sale ratio, 49–52
questions to ask, 18–22
reluctance to prospect, 60–62, 63–65
scenarios, 228–35
Times Square story and, 57–59
ups/downs of selling and, 63–65
Prospect Management System, 23. *See also* Triangle model
avoiding disconnects, 93–94
implementing, 105–7
moving sales cycle forward, 75–77
for multiple products/services, 95–96
relationships and. *See* Relationships
Pushiness, 129–30

Qualifying, 102–4. *See also* Prospecting/
prospects
defined, 40
listening and, 6
questions to ask/not ask, 6
sales process and, 40, 78
Questions to ask
about competition, 162
about status quo, 208–9
about the elephant, 207–9
Cloistered Customers, 159
for closing accounts, 39–43
for customer service, 8, 9
for determining buying stage, 162–64
easy vs. hard, 219–20
excuses for not asking, 9–11
for keeping accounts, 6, 8, 9, 159
for opening meetings, 202–4, 207–9
pre-meeting planning items, 188–89, 191–92
for qualifying customers, 6
simple, for interview, 219–26
for your #1 prospect, 18–22
Ratios. *See* Number(s)
Relationships. *See also* Communication;
Interviewing customers; Meetings
(with decision makers)
asking simple questions and, 219–26
avoiding "...just following up,"
131–32, 133–34
business dynamics, 174–82
call to new referral, 232–34
Cloistered Customers and, 156–59
cultivating allies, 116–17, 125–26
EMPs and, 153–55, 157, 163–64
expanding, 37, 116–19, 131–32, 228–32
IMPs and, 151–52, 157, 163–64
likeability and, 179–80
moving to Next Step, 131–32, 133–34
new, calling without referral, 234–35
not-buying signals and, 134, 135–37
overcoming barriers, 186–87
pressures on decision-makers and, 149–50
prospecting and, 50, 131–32